Huffman

BEYOND
THE
DISTANT
SHADOWS

BEYOND THE DISTANT SHADOWS

PATRICIA DUNAWAY

BETHANY HOUSE PUBLISHERS
MINNEAPOLIS, MINNESOTA 55438
A Division of Bethany Fellowship, Inc.

Copyright © 1984
Patricia Dunaway
All Rights Reserved

Published by Bethany House Publishers
A Division of Bethany Fellowship, Inc.
6820 Auto Club Road, Minneapolis, Minnesota 55438

Printed in the United States of America

Library of Congress Cataloging in Publication Data

Dunaway, Patricia, 1936-
   Beyond the distant shadows.

   I. Title.
RS3554.U4633B4 1984   813'.54   84-18536
ISBN 0-87123-446-7 (pbk.)

DEDICATION

To my husband Jack, who believes in me.

THE AUTHOR

PATRICIA DUNAWAY attended Baylor University and Southwestern Seminary. She has taught fiction writing at Central Oregon Community College for two years. She is married, the mother of three children and they make their home in Bend, Oregon.

CHAPTER 1

Denis Chaumont sighed. He was sixteen years old; the Louisiana darkness was warm and soft; and the horse that pulled the carriage was obligingly slow and plodding. And seated by his side was the most fascinating young woman he'd ever had the pleasure to meet.

He glanced at her for the twentieth time. She was asleep, her head drooping. He moved imperceptibly closer, hoping she might need to rest on his shoulder. *Ah*, he thought, *what hair!* A deep auburn color, it was coiled and looped in such lush profusion that it had taken his breath away at first glance. He considered himself extremely lucky to have been the one she had approached in the livery stable earlier that evening. She had asked if there was someone who would drive her to Greenlea—as if he wouldn't have driven her twice around the world! Yet, even so, Denis had been on the verge of refusing; no one went voluntarily to Greenlea nowadays.

But who could refuse an angel? True, her generous mouth did show a dismaying, non-angelic determination; she had dispelled all his arguments against coming to Greenlea at night. But aside from that, she did have the face of an angel, with creamy white skin and no freckles—at least not any he had been able to see through her veil, which fanned out from the silly little black hat perched on that glorious hair. The veil hadn't been able to conceal her eyes, though. Such beautiful eyes they were too, green and sparkling. And she was a lady as well.

But his own Katy was a lady, he reminded himself, and sighed. If only he were older, they could marry now, instead of waiting as Father Etienne had firmly suggested. The very thought of marriage to Katy, even in the distant future, made

9

him sit up straighter.

His sudden movement wakened the young woman and she stirred, reaching to lift the veil from her face. "Oh, I'm so sorry to have gone to sleep; how terrible of me!"

He smiled shyly, very much aware now that he was the son of a fisherman; she, the daughter of a D'Arcy. "No, not at all, Miss Cole. You've been travelin' a right smart time, what with the steamship from New York City to New Orleans, and then the ferry across the river." He chuckled. "I'll bet you thought it was easier to make the trip down the coast than it was to get ol' Seth to run the ferry."

"You know this Seth, I suppose?"

"I reckon I do. Everyone knows Seth, and they know how Seth loves the bottle, too. You're lucky he was sober enough to bring you over."

"I'm not certain he was," the lady remarked wryly. "I'm very grateful you agreed to drive me to Greenlea; otherwise I can't imagine how I would have managed. It's been some time since I've seen my sister Bethany. She and Dr. Jarrett, her husband, haven't been able to get back to New York very often since they moved here." She straightened the stiff black silk of her mourning dress without noticing his startled response to the names. But he changed the subject.

With gentle, inoffensive curiosity Denis asked, "Have you recently lost a loved one?"

"Yes, my mother."

"Ah, I'm sorry. Was it sudden?"

"No. She was ill for a very long time, over four years. Since I'm unmarried, I was able to be at home and care for her." Then because she had faced the fact long ago, she added simply, "My father, Landrum Cole, died just before she became ill. I was named for him."

"Oh? Your name is Landrum?"

She laughed softly at his question. "I had no brothers, so they called me Landra. I'm really quite proud of being named for him. He was more than a father to me . . ." She trailed off, aware that she was talking too much, that it would be impossible to explain to this curious young man all that Landrum Cole had been to his younger daughter. A man of strong, inner convictions, he had felt keenly the need to share his faith in God with his daughters. Though her mother had quietly set aside her early Catholic upbringing to unite the family in worship, a subtle, invisible division of sorts had existed. Landra, because of her devotion to her father, had followed him in his Protestant beliefs, while Bethany, after her marriage to Adam and the return to Louisiana, had become a devout Catholic. Though the situation was never discussed openly, Marie Cole had been closer to Bethany, as Landra was to her father. Surprisingly, they had been an extremely harmonious family.

Landra thought with longing of her mother and father, each of whom had given so generously of themselves. Her father had never tried to make her into the son he knew he would never have, but had given the best that was in him. His best had been very good, indeed. But he was dead, her mother was dead, and Landra Cole was now coming home.

"You know, Mr. Chaumont— "

"It'd be just fine if you wanted to call me Denis, ma'am."

Landra returned his winsome smile. "Denis, then. It's been so long since I've been home." Her voice lingered on the last word. "New York was never home to me, even though I've lived there since I was fifteen. Father moved us there for business reasons in the spring of 1891, so it's been almost exactly ten years. Ten years is a long time," she said wistfully. "—But I'm boring you with all this."

"Oh no, ma'am," he said quickly. In truth, he could have listened all night to the quiet Yankee voice. But they were very near Greenlea. He frowned. There'd been so many tales about the place. At first it had been just the strangeness of having a doctor who didn't take patients. Called himself a scientist, he did. He was a doctor, wasn't he? Dr. Adam Jarrett. Everyone had been so pleased when Bethany Cole had brought her husband home to the old place to live, and that he was a doctor was even better. Old Dr. Freman was just not able to make his rounds anymore, and some said he could barely see you even if you went to his office.

But the folks soon found Dr. Jarrett wasn't an ordinary doctor. There was the thing about his wife, too. Denis looked at the young woman beside him, realizing again that it was her sister he was thinking of. He crossed himself, and slapped the horse with the reins. "We're almost there." Silently he added, *And what I ought to do is turn around and take you right back.* But he didn't, and soon they were in sight of Greenlea. He reined the horse to a halt.

Landra caught her breath: she was home. "Denis, I'm going to walk the rest of the way."

"But, miss, you'll get your slippers wet. The dew's mighty heavy—"

She had already slipped from the carriage, managing the long skirt of her black dress deftly. She ran a few steps forward into the curved drive that led to the front of the house, then stood transfixed. It was so lovely. There was a faint glow of moonlight on the fine two-story columns that marched six abreast, the huge old cypress door on the main floor, the tall windows on both stories.

The house was constructed of brick painted white, raised more than eight feet on brick piers, precaution against periodic flooding from the mighty Mississippi, which was not far away. The oyster-shell drive crunched under her feet as she ran lightly up to the shadowed veranda. Now she noticed what had not been apparent to her before in the intense pleasure of just being home.

There were no lights. Because of the location, the Coles had found it economically impossible to install gaslights at Greenlea, but always before there had been the soft welcome of lamps or candlelight. Now it was dark, the tall windows black. Eagerly she turned the doorknob, to no avail. She let the huge brass knocker rise and fall several times, but there was no answer. A whippoorwill gave his lonely cry, and Landra heard the welcome sweet song of a mockingbird nearby. But there was no sound from within the house. How could that be? Even if Adam and Bethany were out, surely Beulah was there, and the other servants.

An owl flew through the veranda and out again, setting her heart pounding before she realized what it was. Anxiously she bit her lip, trying to decide what to do. Maybe Beulah was in the old kitchen. How inconvenient it had been to build kitchens apart from the house—the food always got cold taking it from one place to the other. When Landrum Cole had insisted on converting one of the downstairs rooms into a kitchen, Beulah, their cook, had asked if she might live in the old one. Landra shivered; she might as well look there—anything to get away from the silent darkness that whispered of things too frightening to contemplate.

Breathlessly she reached the door of the small building at the rear of the main house and saw a dim light glowing somewhere inside. Instead of reassuring her, it only served to deepen the concern that chilled her, even though the air was warm and heavy, scented with jasmine and magnolia. And then a shape, a hunched form, passed fleetingly in front of the window.

"Beulah—is that you?"

Somehow she knew it was not Beulah. She stood still, unable to breathe or move as the door swung open. There was a candle on the table nearby, dripping and sputtering its life away, but it gave enough light for her to see the man's face—except he had no face!

"What do you want?" The harsh, guttural voice scraped at her nerves. She turned blindly; her only conscious thought was to flee. In her haste she stumbled, falling against the upright support of the porch. Her head struck it squarely, and she clung to it, a small moan involuntarily escaping her lips.

From behind her she heard a step, and that awful, guttural voice saying, "Don't, I—"

Landra, dazed though she was, somehow made her way off the porch and back around the big house to where Denis was waiting anxiously.

"Miss Landra, where in tarnation did you go?" he said, then realized she was all but staggering. "What happened? Are you all right?" With only a moment's hesitation he put an arm around her shoulders, and Landra leaned on him heavily.

"I . . . something frightened me and I fell. . . ." She caught her breath, and put her hand to her forehead. When it came away after a moment she and Denis were both shocked to see the darkish smear of blood in the white glow of moonlight.

"Your head—it's bleeding! Did you hit it on something?" He all but carried her over to the carriage, then helped her carefully into it. "What happened? I'd better get you to a doctor."

Landra looked back at the house, confusion and pain making it hard for her to think. "I . . . my sister—"

"It would seem your folks aren't home." He hesitated, then said, "Maybe I ought to go and see what's up, ma'am. What was it that scared you?" Manfully he straightened and started back toward the house.

She took a deep breath and caught his arm. "No, please don't leave me, Denis. Let's go back into town."

"Are you sure?" He almost hid the note of relief in his voice.

"Yes, yes, I'm sure. Perhaps you could bring me back to-morrow?"

"That I will, if you're up to it, anyway. I think we ought to go straightaway to get that cut on your head looked at." He unwound the reins and gave the horse a smart tap, noticing that she looked back once, quickly. "Ah, Miss Landra, what was it you saw?"

Landra shuddered. "I . . . I'm not sure . . ."

"Was it someone—a man, I mean?"

She hesitated so long he almost asked the question again before her answer, low and unsteady, came. "Yes, it was a man."

"Could it have been your brother-in-law, and he didn't recognize you in the dark?"

"No, it wasn't Adam! It was—" She halted, unwilling to voice what she had seen. Her head hurt, and the whole hideous scene was beginning to blur, to have the quality of a nightmare once the dreamer comes fully awake.

Denis was not to be put off, however. With the tenacity of the young he said gently, persistently, "What did you see, miss?"

"It was a man . . . but he . . . he had no face," whispered Landra.

He muttered something about God in heaven, then said aloud, "But how can a man have no face? Beggin' your pardon, Miss Landra, I'm not disputing your word, but it's mighty dark, and I'm sure you're mistaken." He slapped the horse again, and the creature moved at almost a brisk pace down the narrow road which was lined with moss-draped trees.

The moon was even brighter now, and Landra determinedly fought back the image of that ruined face. The brief glance she'd had was of a vague flatness, pierced by gaping holes which bore little resemblance to human features. But he had been human, he had spoken to her.

Bethany. If that man had something to do with her being gone . . . Landra stifled an exclamation of mingled anguish and exasperation. She should tell Denis to turn around immediately, and go with him to investigate. But she didn't. The thought of the dark, locked house stopped her.

Beth's letters for months had been so strange. There was no doubt in Landra's mind that her sister had written them; always about Adam and Greenlea, they were quite chatty and pleasant. The puzzling, disturbing thing was that while Landra wrote often of their mother's gradual decline, Bethany had made no comment whatever about it. Instead, she had always inquired dutifully about Marie, as though Landra had written nothing. And Beth's last letter, coming after Landra's own informing her sister of their mother's death, was the final, shocking straw, the reason Landra had come home to see for herself what was wrong. There was something dreadfully wrong, and this night's events were far from reassuring. Where were Bethany and Adam? She closed her eyes, unaware that a tiny sigh had escaped her lips.

Denis said softly, "Too bad, Miss Landra, your homecoming had to turn out like this. But we'll get it all straight tomorrow."

"Thank you, Denis; you've been so helpful."

"It's nothing. Mama would be glad to put you up for the night, or as long as you like. There's not much in the way of inns and hotels in Noirville. Unless, of course, you'd like to go back to New Orleans to see a doctor?"

"No, I can't leave now," she said hastily. "I have to find my sister. She and Dr. Jarrett may be on a trip. Yes, that could be it; maybe they've gone on a trip."

"Isn't likely, ma'am."

Something in his tone made her ask, "Why do you say that, Denis?"

"I don't like to say, Miss Landra. It doesn't seem right."

"Please tell me; I'm so worried." She put her hand to her eyes, feeling a throbbing ache behind them.

Denis Chaumont hesitated, then said slowly, "I won't lie; I thought twice before bringing a lady like you out here. There are some pretty awful stories going around about your brother-in-law. You being his wife's sister, I guess I thought you had a right to come to your own home. But I got no right to carry tales to you about your kin. It's best you hear whatever it is from the doctor himself. Gossip is for women, beggin' your pardon."

He was silent then, and Landra sensed he meant what he said and didn't intend to volunteer any more information. She risked one more question. "Denis, do you know my sister?"

"Yes, ma'am," he said reluctantly.

"When did you see her last?"

He didn't look at Landra as he spoke. "I'm not even sure. It's been way over a year since any of us have seen her, Miss Landra, maybe even closer to two."

Over a year! How could that be? "Denis, was she well? How did she look?"

"Ah, like you, like an angel. Only with golden curls." He ducked his head, embarrassed at his own words. "She was always coming round, doing for someone. Like the time she came every day for two weeks when Mrs. Boucher was down, and looked after all those kids—she loved kids, Mrs. Jarrett did; my own little sisters can tell you that." His voice had grown quieter with each word.

"But was she well?" Landra persisted.

Denis was silent for a while before he answered. "As far as I know, ma'am, as far as I know. After all, her husband's a doctor, isn't he? If she was to get sick, he'd look after her, wouldn't he?"

Landra started to say he wasn't that kind of doctor, but she didn't. For she believed with all her heart that Adam would, indeed, take care of Bethany. When he'd announced his decision to leave New York and his fine position in a laboratory there to come to Greenlea, the whole family had objected at first. Then, knowing of Beth's attachment to Greenlea and her obvious delight at the prospect of returning to her home, they all had relented and shared her joy. Not the least important fact was how very much Adam Jarrett loved his beautiful young wife; the move was made in part to please her. Of course, he had felt there was important work to be done on his own and agreed with the move also because of the nearness of the Tulane School of Medicine in New Orleans. *Yes*, thought Landra, *Adam would take care of Bethany*.

Denis pulled the carriage to a halt and bounded down to assist Landra. "I see a light, Miss Landra. The only thing is, I forgot that old Doc Freman hasn't been too well—" He halted as Landra stumbled a little, a slight dizziness making her clutch his shoulder.

"Oh, I'm sorry!"

"It's all right, it's all right," he soothed, his arm around her waist as he helped her through the white picket gate. The door opened as they approached the porch, and a man peered out.

"Who's there? Do you need help?"

"Yes, this lady took a fall and hit her head," said Denis, grateful when he realized the man was not the old doctor but his grandson, Hollis Freman. Although the older folks of the community spoke of his youth as though it were a handicap, Denis was glad to see him; young or not, he was a doctor and any help right now was welcome. "I don't know how bad it is, but she should be looked at."

"Of course. Come in, and I'll have Mrs. Olsen make some tea. How long ago did it happen?"

The two helped Landra into the front room and she sank onto the couch, not even bothering to protest when the young Dr. Freman slipped a needlepoint footstool beneath her feet and a pillow behind her neck. "Put your head back and lie still. I'll get my bag."

She closed her eyes as he moved away, mostly to shut out the sight of Denis' worried expression. "This is terrible; I hate to be such a bother." Like most strong people, she much preferred to take care of others instead of being taken care of. The past long months of caring for her mother, of being in complete charge of a very serious situation only emphasized her present helplessness.

"It's all right," soothed Denis again. "Just take it easy, and the doctor will take care of you." He wasn't so sure his mother would agree. She had set great store by old Doc Freman before he'd gotten too ill to care for patients. The young man they heard rummaging about in the next room was fresh out of medical school, and the rumor was that the old Doc wanted him to stay in Noirville and take over his practice. The only problem was that the people of Noirville weren't so sure they wanted a young whippersnapper telling them what to do, or more importantly, what not to do.

Landra opened her eyes and looked around her at the room, dominated by a large rosewood piano. The piano was imposing; it had to be to dominate the room, filled as it was to overflowing with bric-a-brac and overstuffed Victorian furniture. Just then Dr. Freman, an appropriately serious expression on his face, came in, black bag in hand.

He sat on the opposite end of the ornately carved love seat, took her hand, and felt gently on her wrist for a pulse. "I'm Dr. Freman, Hollis Freman. Does your head hurt?"

Landra put a hand tentatively on her forehead. "I . . . no, not much now. I probably didn't need to come; it's not really very bad."

"Nonsense. Denis did the right thing bringing you here. Let's get it cleaned up and see what we've got." He rummaged in the new black bag at his feet, took out some cotton wool and a bottle of antiseptic. Gently, he wiped away the now dried blood, and Landra watched him.

He was totally engrossed in his task, totally unaware of her scrutiny of him. He was very near her own age, probably no more than a year or two older. The eyes beneath his fair hair were clear and blue, his nose and mouth ordinary when taken singly; but there was a deep cleft in his chin and a handsome set to his square jaw; all added up to an impressive total.

Landra had the strangest feeling that she knew him, that they'd met before. But try as she might, no memory surfaced. When she realized she must have been staring, she smiled a little nervously and said, "I appreciate your help, Dr. Freman."

"Hmm. Glad for something to do. The folks around here have been avoiding me like the plague." He shot a glance at Denis. "Most of them would probably avoid me even if they *had* the plague. They think there isn't anyone like my grandfather."

"He's a good man, a good doctor," put in Denis. "How is he, anyway?"

Hollis Freman finished cleansing the cut on Landra's forehead, and after finding a suitable bandage, made sure it was neat and square on the wound, with bits of tape holding it securely. "He had another stroke and we had to take him to the hospital in New Orleans."

"I'm sorry to hear it," said Denis, "but glad you were here. Miss Landra needed someone. Is it very bad, the cut on her head, I mean?"

"I don't think so. Watch for signs of nausea or undue sleepiness in case of concussion. Did you strike it very hard?"

"No, not really." Landra suddenly felt very weak, and though she tried to keep it from showing, she was not entirely successful.

"Denis," said the young doctor, "you'd better get her to—" He stopped, then said, "Where are you staying, anyway?"

"I—"

Denis interrupted. "She's going to stay with us, at least until we find out some things. Right, Miss Landra?"

Though she usually preferred to make her own decisions, at that particular moment the idea of being cared for was more than Landra could resist. "Yes, Denis, thank you." She allowed Dr. Freman to help her up, grateful for the warm strength of his arm around her as he led her out to the carriage and practically lifted her into it. He was tall, probably six inches taller than she, and this task seemed to present no particular problem for him. "And I thank you as well, Dr. Freman."

"I'm the one who should thank you," he said with a little smile.

"I don't understand."

"You're my first patient, unless you count the kitten that Jenny Fairchild brought in yesterday." A lock of fair hair fell insistently over his broad forehead; he brushed it back, but it refused to stay. "Miss Cole, I really should check on your condition tomorrow."

"I'll see to it, Dr. Freman." Denis climbed into the carriage beside her. "Thanks a lot, and I sure hope your grandpa gets over this one." He clucked to the patient old horse, and they moved away into the night, leaving Landra with a curious feeling of loss.

A short time later Denis pulled the carriage to a halt and assisted Landra to the ground. The house before them was small, the roof sloping over a porch that spanned the front. It bore no resemblance to her childhood home in style or grandness, but the bright light that spilled from its windows cheered Landra after the dark unwelcome of Greenlea.

"Mama!" Denis called. "Mama—I've brought a visitor!"

A tall, slim woman with thick braids wound around her head came out and stood watching as Denis and Landra stepped onto the porch. She smiled, and Landra knew where Denis had gotten his own winsome ways. As they drew nearer, Landra could see that her dark hair was threaded liberally with silver and there were lines of care about her eyes. Mrs. Chaumont held out both hands, and as if it were the most natural thing in the world, Landra put her own in them. "I'm Landra Cole."

"Welcome to my home," Mrs. Chaumont said simply.

"Thank you. I hope it isn't too much of an imposition, but Denis said—"

Mrs. Chaumont smiled fondly at her son. "Denis all the time brings someone, but not often like you!" She touched Landra's shoulder, felt the richness of the black silk, a question in her kind eyes.

Denis stood watching, and Landra was grateful when he explained quietly, "Miss Cole lost her mother not long ago, Mama, and when I took her to her home there was no one there." He saw that she noticed the stark whiteness of the bandage at Landra's temple. Not wanting to breach a confidence but knowing his mother would certainly wonder, he added, "She fell, and hit her head while we were there, so I took her to Doc Freman."

Mrs. Chaumont clucked her sympathy. "What did he say? Are you all right?"

"Yes, of course." But suddenly Landra felt an almost overwhelming fatigue, and she swayed involuntarily.

Mrs. Chaumont put an arm around her shoulders. "Come in, come in. I'll make a room ready. You need rest. Denis, bring her things."

"Okay, Mama." He went down the walk whistling, knowing that Mama would take care of the situation. She always did. Maybe there was still time to take Katy for a walk.

The inside of the Chaumont house was simply furnished, with odd bits of furniture. The chairs in the kitchen had open seats laced with rawhide and covered with bright yellow calico pads. Landra sat in one of these as she watched her hostess take a kettle from the stove and brew a pot of tea. She heard a stifled giggle from the doorway and turned to see three little girls peeking around. They were like stairsteps, and their bright eyes watched her curiously.

"Miss Cole, meet Jeannette, Joyeuse, and Jolie." All three did a bobbing imitation of a curtsey. Mrs. Chaumont smiled, then said, "You girls go back to bed, you hear? And don't let me catch you up again. Jeannette, you sleep with Jolie tonight."

They disappeared in a giggling flurry, and Mrs. Chaumont shook her head in exasperation as she set a cup before Landra. "It's not easy raising children alone."

Landra wanted to ask about her husband, but decided against it. She raised the steaming cup to her lips, puzzled at the tea's strange fragrance. "What is this?" she asked.

"Just a tisane—tea. It's good for you, help you sleep."

Landra doubted whether she would need help, and when she had drunk the strange-tasting liquid she felt almost nerveless. She tried without success to keep from nodding. Ruefully she said, "I went to sleep in the carriage with Denis, too. You're both going to think I'm ill-mannered."

"That's the furthest thing from my mind. For you to face the disappointment of your folks being away, and the accident—" She stopped, her eyes so kind and gentle it made Landra's throat tight. "I'll wager you've come a long way today."

"Yes, as soon as the ship docked, I came over from New Orleans. I had hoped . . ." She trailed off. It was no use going into detail about her hopes that somehow when she got to Greenlea, Beth would explain away her fears.

As though she knew it was no time for questions or explanations, Mrs. Chaumont said, "Come along. I'll get your room

ready while you prepare yourself for bed. You're much too tired
to be trying to carry on a conversation."

She allowed the woman to lead her down a narrow hallway,
which bisected the house, and into a small room—neat, but
bearing unmistakable signs of a little girl's occupancy. There
was a row of dolls on the chest and tiny rosebud print curtains
at the window. Landra washed the grime from her face and
hands while her hostess changed the bed linens and turned
them back invitingly. "There," she said, "slip into your nightgown, and in the morning things will look much better, Miss
Cole. They always do, you know."

Mrs. Chaumont quietly left the room then, taking the lamp
with her. Weary beyond words, Landra crept between the sheets.
She was almost asleep when she remembered the formless face.
She shut her eyes tightly, but the face was still there. With a
little shudder she rolled to the edge of the small bed and slipped
to the floor; in the habitual posture of childhood she knelt, face
to the sweet-smelling sheets, hands clasped above.

"Oh, Lord, I'm so afraid. Please help me not to be afraid . . .
help me to be calm and not fly off in all directions. Lord, you
know me; you know I can't always keep my temper, and I do
things when I ought to stop, and think . . . and pray." Her whispered words caught in her throat and broke. "Please, God, help
me to find Bethany." She was silent for a long time; her prayers
often, if not always, left her with the troubled feeling there was
something missing. Finally she rose and slipped beneath the
sheets. Her sleep, when she lay down again, was deep and
dreamless, without the hideous remembrance of the man in the
old kitchen.

CHAPTER 2

The sun was bright and high when she woke to find herself in a strange place. Her head felt better than she had expected; only if she moved quickly, which she avoided after the first time, did she feel pain. Dr. Freman's bandage was still firmly in place. The thought of the earnest young doctor brought a smile to her lips. *He was really quite—* A knock at the door interrupted her musing and she quickly pulled the covers about her, although her high-necked nightgown was quite modest.

"Yes," she called out, "who is it?"

A sweet voice answered: "Jeannette, and I've brought coffee. You would like some?"

"Yes, thank you, come in," said Landra. She sat up and touched her feet to the floor as the child opened the door.

"No, no! Don't get up. Mama says you're to have your rolls and coffee in bed."

The words were quite authoritative, and Landra obediently lay back. She risked a small smile, however, at the sight of the speaker. This was the oldest of the trio, about eleven, with a pretty, heart-shaped face. Her hair was long, dark, and loose, her brown eyes alight with interest in the unexpected visitor.

She set the tray carefully on Landra's lap. Landra noticed with appreciation that the buns were hot and smelled very good. She buttered one, letting Jeannette go on with her frank appraisal, impressed that the child, though she glanced at the bandage, tactfully refrained from commenting.

"Mama says you've come all the way from New York. How?"

"I came on a very large steamship, Jeannette."

"Ahhh," Jeannette sighed. "Someday, I, too, will go on a very large boat, to . . . to everywhere!"

22

Landra laughed at the child's positive exuberance as she sipped the strong, hot coffee. How pleasant it was in this girl's small room, with the bright summer sunlight splashing in the windows. She wanted to forget the endless months spent nursing her mother, and last night . . . She offered a roll to Jeannette, who took it. They ate in companionable silence, Landra putting off the moment when she must face whatever the morning had to offer. It was nothing good, she was sure. "Here, Jeannette, will you take this back to your mother, and tell her thank you for me?"

Jeannette hopped off the bed and took the tray with another of the free Chaumont smiles. She looked at Landra closely. "You don't look like Miss Bethany much, but you're awfully pretty, anyway."

"You know my sister, then?" Landra asked quickly.

"Oh, yes'm. She used to give me books and help me read. I love Miss Bethany," Jeannette finished shyly. "Only, it's been a long time since I saw her."

"Why, Jeannette?"

"Mama says—"

"Jeannette! You stop bothering Miss Cole, you hear?" At the sound of her mother's voice Jeannette took the tray and fled.

Thoughtfully, Landra put on the black silk, wishing she could wear something light and soft and bright, like the morning outside. Denis Chaumont and his mother were waiting for her when she entered the kitchen.

"Good morning," said Mrs. Chaumont. "You slept well, I hope? And your head, does it hurt?"

Landra responded easily to the warmth in her voice. "Why, no, as a matter of fact, it seems to be fine. I slept very well, and I feel perfectly all right, except I'm anxious to get out to Greenlea."

"I'm ready whenever you are, Miss Landra," Denis assured her.

"And there's no need to be afraid, Miss Cole. My Denis will look after you."

"Afraid, Mrs. Chaumont? What do you mean? Did Denis tell you about last night?" The older woman nodded. "Then can you tell me anything more, anything that might help me understand the situation before I go?"

She looked from mother to son, who in turn looked at each

other. In the silence Landra was acutely conscious of the homely room around them. The whitewashed walls, the wide plank floor with small, bright rag rugs scattered about, the pump at the sink, a fly which repeatedly buzzed at the open window . . . the special scents of a May morning.

But she had to prompt them again before either spoke. "Please, can you?"

Mrs. Chaumont sighed. "Denis and me, we talked it over. Now that my man's gone . . ." She paused, crossed herself, and went on. "Well, me and Denis always talk. And we both think it should come from him." At Landra's questioning frown, Mrs. Chaumont added in explanation, "Dr. Jarrett."

Landra could see Mrs. Chaumont believed what she said; and perhaps, after all, they were right. Adam was the one to tell her, whatever it was. "All right. Denis, could we leave right away? If you don't have anything planned, that is."

"Oh, no. Me and the horse are yours!"

"Denis!" His mother shook her head. "What can a mother do with such a son?" she asked Landra, who saw the fierce pride in her eyes.

Landra saw with a sinking heart that Greenlea looked different in the brightness of morning. Last night's moonlight had graciously hidden the peeling paint and the ugly, encroaching mold on the lower bricks. Her mother had always insisted it be painted yearly. She would never have allowed neglect such as this and, Landra was sure, neither would Bethany.

"Oh, Denis! It looks as though no one cares, as if—" She hesitated, then said slowly, unwillingly, "As if no one lives here who cares about the place."

Even as she said it her anxiety deepened, for she knew how very much Bethany did care. Landra rebelled at the thoughts which pushed unbidden into her mind; thoughts which said plainly that Bethany would, if she were here, have seen lovingly and painstakingly to the upkeep of Greenlea. Suddenly, she could wait no longer to go inside to see if her sister was there, and if not, to find out where she was.

Denis, a frown on his face, halted the rig in front of the curved veranda. "I'll go in with you, ma'am," he said.

"There's no need for that, Denis," she said with a false assurance which prompted her to add, "But I'd appreciate it if you'd wait . . . if it isn't too much trouble—"

"I wasn't planning to leave, Miss Landra; don't you worry about that!"

She smiled at the serious expression on his rather homely young face. "Thank you, Denis." As she started to step from the carriage, he gallantly leaped out and handed her down. "You're quite a gentleman, do you know that?"

He blushed to the tips of his ears, grinning at her praise. Denis nonchalantly leaned against the far column as Landra walked to the double doors. Out of the corner of his eye, he followed her movements. He felt a pang of sympathy for her, wished there was some way he could help. Since his father's death, he had developed a fine sense of protectiveness for his mother and sisters in particular, and all women in general. He felt it keenly now for Landra, and wished with a sudden fierceness that he were older.

The doors showed the inevitable ravages of the semi-tropical climate. This same climate was responsible for the lush greenness all around, but without constant care, exposed wood deteriorated quickly. Landra touched the roughened surface briefly before she took hold of the brass knocker and let it fall. This time she would not give up until someone came. To her surprise, there was no need to knock again. Just as her hand lifted, the door opened, and she looked up into the face of a young man.

"Yes?" he said, courteously enough, though Landra could tell it was mere courtesy with no real welcome. Who was he?

In the brief moments before she spoke, she took in the fact that he was slim and very tall, perhaps six feet two or so, his dark blond hair curling about his ears with mutton-chop whiskers edging his jaws; his eyes were clear and hazel. There was nothing remarkable about him except his clothes. The fine coat and trousers he wore were rich dark brown and fawn colored, respectively, and tailored very well. He looked much like many of the well-to-do young suitors that had come in droves to court her sister Bethany, and would, if circumstances had been different, have come to court her as well. She impatiently brushed these thoughts aside.

"I'm Landra Cole, and I've come to see my sister Bethany," she said with as much quiet dignity as she could muster.

She was quite unprepared for the change that came over the young man before her. His face turned pale; Landra saw with alarm that he had to grasp the edge of the door to support himself. His eyes were staring at her face, and she raised the veil, as though she knew he wanted her to. "You, you're Bethany's . . . Mrs. Jarrett's sister?"

"Yes, I am. May I come in?" Anxiety made her voice sharper than it normally was, and the young man reacted to it immediately.

"No! I . . . that is, Dr. Jarrett isn't expecting you," he said, looking back into the dark interior of the house.

"I can see that, but it isn't my fault; I wrote, several times. Look, I've come all the way from New York to see my sister." She felt the anger rising in her, welcomed it, for this preposterous young man had inched the door almost closed until there was only room for him to stand. As impossible as it seemed, it appeared to be true that he did not intend to let her in.

"Will you tell me who you are?" she asked.

"I'm Lucas Delacroix, Dr. Lucas Delacroix," he said. Landra heard a scornful grunt from the end of the veranda. Denis stepped out, and Dr. Delacroix saw him for the first time. "And who are you?" he asked, the frown deepening between his eyes.

"I'm Denis Chaumont, Miss Cole's driver," Denis answered, drawing himself up. "And I think you'd better let her in! It doesn't seem too friendly, the way you're treating her." Even in her agitation Landra heard the belligerence of reckless youth.

For an answer, however, Dr. Delacroix firmly closed the door behind him. "Now look, Chaumont, whoever you are, I should think you'd realize you have no business giving me orders. In fact, you've no business here at all," he added as he unbuttoned the beautifully tailored coat and placed his hands on his hips, the aggressiveness in his manner unmistakable.

"Maybe not, but Miss Cole has. And you'd better let her in if you know what's good for you," said Denis, his voice almost, not quite, cracking, as he came to stand protectively beside Landra.

"See here, don't threaten me!" Dr. Delacroix took a step toward Denis, and Landra realized with dismay that the two were very near an actual fight.

"Please, don't! Denis, it's all right." She laid a hand on his arm, and he stepped back reluctantly. Landra turned her attention to Dr. Delacroix. Perhaps she was going about the whole thing in the wrong way, she thought. After all, it was simply a basic fact that honey was better than vinegar, as the old saying went. So, her eyes screened by long, dark lashes, she said quietly, "Dr. Delacroix, surely you can understand my concern for my sister. My—our mother died only last month, and I've heard nothing that makes sense either from Bethany or Dr. Jarrett. Please"—here she raised those emerald eyes, made even more jewel-like by the sparkle of real tears—"please tell Dr. Jarrett I'm here!"

His blustery attitude gone, Dr. Delacroix softened visibly as he stared into her face. "But he isn't here; he's in New Orleans."

"Then may I come in and wait? At least until he returns?" The fact that he had said absolutely nothing about Bethany made her even more determined to get inside the house.

"I'm sorry, but I'm not sure when that will be," he said, the stubborn scowl returning to his face.

"Dr. Delacroix, this is my home. I was born here. It's been ten years since I was here last, and I want very much to—" She allowed her real longing to creep into her voice, and was gratified to see his expression soften, a look of sympathy replacing the scowl.

He opened the door, and stood aside for her. Denis started to follow, but Dr. Delacroix said definitely, "If you don't mind, please wait for Miss Cole in the carriage."

"But—" said Denis.

"It's all right, Denis, really it is." Landra turned to him. "If it isn't too much trouble, could you wait, at least until I find out something?"

"Surely you're not thinking I'd go off and leave you?" He eyed Dr. Delacroix with open suspicion. "I'll be right here if you need me."

Landra smiled her thanks and followed Lucas Delacroix into the dim interior of Greenlea, ignoring the small pang of anxiety she felt at the sound of the door closing behind them.

Her anxiety gave way to dismay as she became accustomed to the dimness. There was the lovely curve of the half-circle stairway which led up and around and down again; but to her right, in the drawing room, she could see white-draped mounds. Each piece of furniture was covered with sheets, and the heavy rose-colored draperies, such a source of pride to her mother, were drawn tightly at each of the tall windows, letting only small slivers of light into the large, airless room. Bethany had spoken so often of returning here; of how this place, with all its happy memories, would be hers and Adam's home. It was a far cry from anyone's home now. No one lived here, not the way Bethany had meant.

Lucas Delacroix was carefully removing a sheet from a dark red velvet settee, his back toward Landra. When he turned to face her she said, her voice so low he could scarcely hear the words, "Doctor, where is my sister?"

He cleared his throat and said, "I have to check on things in the lab. If you'll just wait here, when Dr. Jarrett returns I'll tell him you're here."

He was obviously going to ignore her question. Frowning, she said, "The lab?"

"Why, yes, didn't you know? Dr. Jarrett maintains a laboratory here at Greenlea. I'm his . . . assistant." Although he tried to hide it, there was a hint of resentment in his last words. He hesitated, then added, "It would be best if you'd wait here." She started to protest but he turned abruptly and left, walking in the direction of the rear of the house where Landrum Cole's study had once been.

The echo of his footsteps died away and she stood uncertainly, filled equally with anger and apprehension. How dare he treat her like an unwelcome guest in her own home? Telling her to wait, as he might an unruly child? He probably wasn't much older than she was! Her jaw set rebelliously, she took a step in the direction he'd gone. But she stopped at the remembrance of the man in the old kitchen the night before; it was possible that *he* might be in the laboratory.

With a sigh of resentment at her own cowardice, she retreated to the settee which Lucas Delacroix had uncovered. Her family had taken little of the fine old funiture with them when they'd moved to New York. Landrum Cole had been willing enough, but Marie had said the things belonged here at Greenlea and nowhere else . . . for Bethany. She had arranged for a widowed aunt to live in the house, saying she didn't want to think of it being empty.

Even at fifteen, Landra had seen the pain it caused her mother to leave Greenlea. When she'd asked her about it, Marie Cole had replied gently, "A woman follows her husband, Landra. This move is important to him, and he is more important to me than Greenlea. You'll understand when you're older. Besides, Bethany loves it as I do, and perhaps she will marry soon and live here. She's said many times she's determined to, and I pity the man who tries to change her mind." Adam hadn't tried. He had been quite willing to come to Greenlea to live.

Landra waited as long as she could, but as the minutes ticked by she became increasingly impatient. She rose and tiptoed into the hall. There was no sound. At the foot of the stairway she stopped, still listening, angry that she would have to do so, but vaguely aware of the need for caution.

By some standards Greenlea was quite small, a scaled-down version of some of the larger plantation houses, such as Elkhorn, whose lands bordered Greenlea. Where Elkhorn had probably twenty bedrooms and was three stories high, Greenlea had only six bedrooms upstairs, four of them fairly small. Then there was the master bedroom, which had been her parents' and was surely Bethany and Adam's now . . . and the nursery, which Bethany had spoken so hopefully about. So many of her letters used to end with, "When our first son is born. . . ." But there had been no sons, only a series of miscarriages that threatened Bethany's life time and time again.

Slowly Landra began to climb the stairs. They were wide and perfectly spaced, making a graceful ascent or descent not only possible but inevitable. Memories flooded her unwilling mind. How she had longed to be twenty instead of ten, to wear a daring, decollette dress of fine silk and flirt with the scores of dashing young men who flocked to Greenlea. Even at sixteen Bethany had charmed them all.

At the top of the stairs she saw the familiar H-shaped hallway. To the left were the small bedrooms, two of which she and Bethany had occupied. They had each had a room, but more often than not they ended up together in one or the other, muffling the late night giggles that brought shouts from their father. It was to these rooms she went first, unconsciously putting off the moment when she would have to go into *their* room. Each was almost clinically neat. The beds were stripped, their handmade canopies gone, giving them a pitiful, naked look. How she'd loved those canopies! The delicate crocheted scrollwork above her head had been the last thing she'd seen on so many long evenings when the sky was still light. Her mother had believed young girls needed an abundance of rest—beauty sleep, she'd called it. There were no personal possessions in any of the rooms except for the one on the very end, where she found a black jacket, a couple of white shirts, and a pair of black boots in the closet. Landra frowned. Was it possible they belonged to Dr. Delacroix? She could see little else in the room to indicate who its owner might be.

Slowly Landra closed the door, walked back to the cross-bar

of the H-shaped hallway, and stood before the huge, heavy door of the room that had been her parents' and which now belonged to her sister and her husband. She glanced over her shoulder as though she thought someone might be watching, as though she was about to do something that was wrong. They had been taught never to enter their parents' bedroom without knocking. Even in her childish, innocent mind, Landra had known it was something more than simple courtesy; something secret, mystical, and absolutely enticing. With a sudden, rebellious resolve, she reached for the knob, but the sound of the door downstairs opening and closing made her spin around, and then her heart stopped. It was Adam. Softly, she tiptoed over to the railing and sank almost to the floor, looking through the smooth white spindles. From there she could barely hear their words, and she pressed close to catch them.

"—told her to come back, but she insisted on coming in. She's in the drawing room—"

"Couldn't you have put her off some way? I thought you realized how careful we have to be!" Adam quieted then and went on talking as he and Lucas walked toward the drawing room, but Landra couldn't hear. Suddenly she was aware of how much like earlier days this scene was. Scores of times she had crouched in almost this exact spot, watching the adults below, longing desperately to be one of them.

Slowly she rose, knowing that when they did not find her in the drawing room, they would come looking for her. At the top step she paused, and took a deep breath. Then she drew herself up proudly, glad she was an unfashionably tall five-foot-seven. With all the grace her mother had drilled into her, she descended the stairs, aware that the two men had come out of the drawing room and stood watching her.

Lucas Delacroix's thin, bony face was a study of contradictions. He was obviously uncomfortable that he had not followed Adam's orders, which had been to allow no one into the house; he was also watching Landra with reluctant admiration.

Adam Jarrett's expression was not as obvious. Landra stood at the foot of the stairs, waiting for him to speak, to come over to her—*something*—but he did not. At first glance she thought he was just as she remembered. He and Lucas Delacroix were approximately the same height, but Adam Jarrett was not as slender. A solid, powerfully-built man, he stood with his large hands clenched at his sides. Landra was unable to keep her eyes from his face. His black, wavy hair sprang with a life of its own back from his forehead, framing black, penetrating eyes.

He was dressed in black, as Landra was. Briefly, irrelevantly, she thought they were a fine pair of crows. But it was only a defense mechanism, a device to keep her from facing the unpleasant reality of the present. What had he said to Dr. Delacroix? *Couldn't you have put her off in some way?*

She was acutely aware of his antagonism, and in a desperate attempt to counteract it said, quite calmly, considering her inner state, "It's good to see you, Adam. I've come to visit—and it would seem that Bethany is on a trip—" She smiled, though at his expression she felt like doing anything but.

"A trip?" His voice was a hollow echo. "Who told you that?"

"Why, no one, I just supposed—"

"You just supposed," he said, repeating her words again, his tone still flat and peculiar sounding. With his eyes squeezed shut, the fine, high color of his face replaced by an ashen pallor, his hands hanging loosely at his sides, he looked absolutely alarming.

Landra caught her breath and took a step toward him, her hand outstretched. "Adam, what is it? Tell me!"

A quick, amazing change came over him then. He straightened, and took the hand Landra had extended. "Forgive me, Landra. I'm behaving abominably. Of course Bethany is gone on a trip, an extended one, I'm afraid. Surely she wrote you?"

Landra spoke slowly, trying to conceal her bewilderment at his behavior, "The last letter I got said nothing about a trip. In fact, it was very confusing, considering—"

He cut her off with a polite smile as he said, "Well, I'm terribly sorry about the mix-up. Can't imagine how it happened, can you, Lucas?" Adam turned to the man beside him, who did not answer, only continued to study the toe of his boot as though it didn't belong there. "At any rate, it's a shame you must leave after just arriving."

"Leave? But Adam, I came to—" She halted, confused. His tone had held a light, false note that upset her far more than his gruff manner of a moment before. The house was obviously closed; there were no servants in evidence, and she wondered suddenly how the two men before her managed. Now she was absolutely certain something was very wrong. Bethany wouldn't leave Adam for an extended trip which, if Adam were to be believed, was nowhere near over. Either her sister and this man were in deep trouble, or something had happened to her.

Uncertainly Landra looked into his eyes, trying to fathom the expression she saw there. His brows were not as heavy as one might expect from the thick unruliness of his hair, and they were well shaped over his dark eyes. She stared at his face; the high cheekbones, almost Indian-like, the wide forehead. It was his mouth that dismayed her—it was hard, compressed, almost as though it were carved of stone. Before, there had always been a mobility, a vital sense of aliveness; that was gone now. Something had happened to change him from the inside out.

CHAPTER 3

It was Lucas Delacroix who broke the endless silence by clearing his throat nervously. In an instant Landra decided there was nothing to be gained by delicately skirting the issue at hand. She had always been inclined to be dismayingly direct, even as a child. Her mother had despaired of teaching her the socially accepted patterns of behavior; Landra simply ignored them unless she thought them sensible—which was, unfortunately, seldom. She took a deep breath and said, "Adam, you're keeping something from me, and I want to know what it is. This is not at all like Bethany. She never even answered my letter telling her about Mother's death." She paused, and could not keep herself from adding, "*You* never wrote." The words came out pitifully small, and Landra was angry with herself for the sound of them. It was just that she knew her mother had been ecstatic when Bethany had married this man, and had loved him lavishly, like a son.

He knew it too, and she could see the pain that flashed across his set face. For the first time he really looked at her, at the somber black dress and veil. "She—Marie is dead?" he said haltingly. "I'm sorry, I didn't know. Her heart . . . was it her heart?"

Landra nodded. "You didn't know? But my letters—"

"I never received them." He had recovered completely, and he said with a cool courtesy that appalled her, "Please accept my condolences. It's unfortunate that you've come so far at such a time, but I'll make all the necessary arrangements for your return to New York as soon as possible"

"I'm not going back."

As though he hadn't heard her words, he said, "I'll find a

33

place for you in town until your reservations can be made."

"You're not listening, Adam, " she said doggedly. "I'm not going back! I can see what has to be done, even if you can't. Dr. Delacroix, will you tell Denis I would appreciate it very much if he would bring in my things? I intend to set this house to rights, and you must send for Bethany at once, Adam."

Adam's cold voice said quickly, definitely, "You are assuming a great deal, Landra. It's impossible for Bethany to return, just as it's impossible for you to stay here. You must leave at once."

"Adam, I—" But he was already grasping her elbow firmly and opening the door. She started to plead with him but something held her back; the thought of begging galled her. She allowed him to propel her out the door, where a very anxious Denis waited.

"Are you all right, Miss Landra?"

"Yes, Denis, I'm fine." To Adam she said, "You're being terribly unfair. I don't understand . . . please help me to understand." Her voice dropped to a whisper. "Where is Bethany?"

He withdrew his hand from her arm, then passed it slowly over his eyes. She had to lean toward him to catch his next words. "Bethany is gone."

"But where, Adam, *where*?"

"I can't tell you now. All I can do is ask that you be patient, and trust me. I'll tell you everything as soon as I can."

"If you won't tell me where she is, at least tell me why she left. Can you do that?" His eyes met hers for a second, then veered away. "Does it have anything to do with that poor man I saw in the old kitchen last night? Are you treating him? Does he have anything to do with her leaving?"

He turned abruptly and went back into the house, leaving Landra with tears of frustration in her eyes. She looked up as Dr. Delacroix came out, closing the door behind him.

"Miss Cole, maybe I can help. Dr. Jarrett has been under a great deal of pressure lately. If you'll just try to understand—"

Landra interrupted him almost wildly. "I understand one thing! You're keeping something from me, and—" She checked herself, realizing she would have to find out what she had to know somewhere else because neither of these two men were willing, or perhaps even able, to tell the truth for reasons totally incomprehensible to her.

"Denis, will you take me back to town, please?" To the anxious young doctor before her she said, "Dr. Delacroix, tell Adam—Dr. Jarrett—that I'll see him again before . . . before I leave."

"Certainly, Miss Cole."

He stood watching as Denis helped her into the carriage, and Landra had the feeling he watched them until they were out of sight. Denis did not speak, for the simple reason that he didn't have the faintest notion of what to say, and Landra was grateful. The horse seemed to have but one gait—the extremely slow plod he'd exhibited the night before. She had ample time to sort out her thoughts and decide what to do next. Somehow she believed Adam when he'd said he never got the news of her mother's death. The surprise and shock on his face had been genuine, and if that was so, then it was up to Landra to find out what had happened to all those letters she'd sent.

She searched her memory. How had the mail always come? Not delivered . . . no, there was a small post office in town, and—of course! Sam'l. It had been the duty of the old Negro man she could only remember as Sam'l to go into town each day and check their box. He had been very old even then, and part of the family all her life. She said urgently to Denis, "Do you know an old man called Sam'l? It's very important!"

"Sam'l. Let me see . . . what's his last name?"

"Why, I don't know, he worked for us all my life; but nobody ever called him anything but Sam'l."

"Worked for you? Was he a nigger?"

Landra bit her lip. She had almost forgotten the word; it had not been a part of her vocabulary even when she had lived here. She was also struck by the sudden realization that no one ever knew a Negro's last name, as though, if he had one at all, it was of no real importance. "I'm sorry I can't tell you his last name, but it's urgent that I find him and talk to him."

"Sure thing. If he's the one I'm thinking about, he lives over in Low Woods."

"Will you take me there?"

Denis reined the horse in sharply. "To nigger-town? *You?*"

"Don't use that word—"

"I'm sorry, Miss Landra. But I can't take you there!"

"Then I'll find someone who will."

"Beggin' your pardon, ma'am," Denis began slowly, for he could see she meant what she said, "but wouldn't it be better if I dropped you off at the house, and you wait there 'til I can go and find Sam'l? Look, Miss Landra, I said I'd take care of you, and it looks like you need it! No offense, but you can't . . . a lady just wouldn't go down to Low Woods like that."

"Denis, if I'm a lady, I'll still be one no matter where I go," Landra said. "Will you take me, or do I have to get someone else?"

Appalled at her determination, Denis was silent for a few moments, thinking it was a good thing his Katy wasn't as headstrong as the young woman beside him.

Troubled, Landra leaned her head against the seat and closed her eyes. "You don't approve of me, do you, Denis?"

For Denis it was the perfect opportunity for studying her before he answered. From the shining auburn hair massed on her head to the dark fringe of eyelash that rested on slightly violet shadows beneath, her rather elegant (to him, at least) nose, the faintly pink curve of generous mouth and firm chin (his gaze rested only briefly on her shapeliness—after all, she was a lady), his eyes swept to the toes of her slender black shoes and back up again. "Ah, no, Miss Landra. You can't say I don't approve of you. I surely do!"

The fervent warmth of his tone made her open her eyes quickly. "But I didn't mean—" She stopped, aware she couldn't go on without acknowledging she'd divined his thoughts.

Aware he'd been rather forward, Denis said, "Miss Landra, I just can't take you to Low Woods. But I will take you to Doc Freman, and let him take another look at you. If he says you're all right, maybe then I'll . . . well, we'll see." He knew he was being evasive, and he also knew she knew. But he was grateful when she didn't protest. As he clucked to the horse he added, "I'm going to have to leave you for a bit at the doctor's if you don't mind. Mama will have my hide if I don't see to the boat."

"Denis! I've been taking you from your work. I'm sorry."

"It's all right, really it is. There's not much going on right now, anyway, because the boat's in drydock for repairs." He smiled timidly. "I just wanted to help you if I could."

"You've been very helpful. I can't imagine what I would have done without you and your family."

He shrugged, and they rode in silence until he drew up in front of Dr. Freman's neat white two-story house. "I'll go in with you."

"No, that's not necessary; you go on and see to your boat. It isn't far to your house and I can walk after I've seen Dr. Freman. And, Denis, thank you again."

"I really haven't done all that much, Miss Landra," the young man said, a troubled look on his face. "I guess if you're still fixed on going to Low Woods, I'll take your stuff back to the house."

"I'd appreciate it. And don't worry about me," she said with a bright smile. "I promise I won't do anything foolish." He nodded, then slapped the reins on the old horse's back and Landra watched as he moved away. Resolutely she walked up the brick path and knocked on Dr. Freman's door.

When he answered she felt the same shock of recognition she had the night before, but instead of voicing it she said, "Dr. Freman, I need help."

"Well, you've come to the right place!" He smiled, delighted. The unruly lock of fair hair was dangling on his broad forehead again, and he swept it back. "Come in, come in. Mrs. Olsen is just fixing tea, won't you have some?"

"No, I—" Landra stopped, suddenly aware that insisting he take her, or find someone to take her to Low Woods was really presumptuous; she should at least try to be courteous, if not patient. "Yes, Dr. Freman, thank you, I will." She followed him into the parlor, a little startled when he shouted, "Mrs. Olsen, bring another glass of tea, please!"

When he sat opposite her on one of the matching love seats, he said apologetically, "She's very hard of hearing. Now, how is your head? Have you had any pain, dizziness, or nausea?"

"No, no, and no," she said, smiling at his earnestness. "I'm fine, really. It's not about my head that I've come; that was Denis' idea. He . . . I wanted him to take me somewhere, and he wouldn't."

"Why, I can't imagine; Denis strikes me as a very helpful young man—" He was interrupted by a roly-poly woman with faded blond hair, carrying a tray with two tall frosty glasses of tea, lemon stuck on the side and a sprig of fresh mint perched on the ice.

Her expression was intensely curious. "I've brought the tea for you and your guest, Dr. Freman."

"Yes, thank you very much. Mrs. Olsen, this is Landra Cole." While she stood, tray still in hand, he added, "Just put it right there," he indicated with a wave of his hand. She saw that he wasn't going to volunteer any more information so put the tray on the table, the look of disappointment on her face barely disguised.

As soon as she had left the room, Hollis Freman leaned forward. "Now tell me what the problem is, and where you need to go."

Landra couldn't keep a tiny smile from her lips. He was so earnest, so intense, so . . . handsome. She felt drawn to him, to his warmth. He barely knew her, and yet he seemed to care in a very real way. It was an appealing trait in a man, she decided. With an effort she brought her rather unruly thoughts in line. "I want to go to Low Woods, Dr. Freman," she said, plunging right in.

He pursed his lips in a silent whistle. "I see." For a moment Landra thought she was in for another bout of persuasion but he merely said, "You need to find someone, I take it."

"Exactly!" She hesitated, then said, "Will you . . . can you take me there? Or find someone who will—"

"Of course I will. Drink your tea, and I'll go and hitch up the horse. Be back in a jiffy." Before Landra could frame a grateful reply he was gone, leaving her in the quietness of the elegantly cluttered room. He really was a marvel—no questions, no argument; he just saw she needed help, and was willing to give it.

She found that the cold, strong tea was what she had wanted without knowing it, and was just finishing when Hollis Freman returned. "I can't tell you how grateful I am. Surely you must have many things to do."

"Don't you believe it," he said with a grin. "I'm remarkably free. The people around here probably won't trust me even to lance their carbuncles until I'm an old graybeard. That's hard on my career, but it leaves me free to pursue other interests. Ma'am, your carriage awaits." He made a sweeping little bow, fair hair dangling.

Almost bemused, Landra rose and followed him outside. The smart carriage had a fringed top, and she was glad, for the sun was quite warm now. As they came nearer to the small settlement made up exclusively of black families, Landra saw that the houses were huddled together, almost without exception unpainted and in need of repairs. But here and there someone had built little fences around clean-swept yards, and the chickens clucking and pecking around the open doors looked well enough fed.

They had seen no one but children up till now, their eyes wide with curiosity. Then a slim, attractive young woman about the same height as Landra came out of one of the houses. "Is there somethin' I can hep you with?" There was no hint of subservience in her tone, merely a civility that seemed entirely natural.

Gratefully Landra said, "Why, yes, thank you. I'm Landra Cole. You might remember my mother—Marie D'Arcy Cole—and my sister, Bethany?"

"Yes'm, I do."

Landra wondered briefly if it was her own overcharged imagination, or was there really a change in the young woman's expression at the mention of Bethany? "I need to find a man who worked for my family, a man named Sam'l. Can you help me?"

"Sure. He live in the last house, straight down yonder. Been there for 'bout six-seven months, ever since Dr. Jarrett let him go. After all those years . . ." She trailed off, stifling the bitterness in her voice with an effort. Nodding curtly she said, "Well, I hope you find him," then turned and went back into her tiny house.

In a subdued voice Landra said to Dr. Freman, who had been silent during the exchange, "I guess I'd forgotten how it is between . . . them and us. It's different up north."

He nodded thoughtfully. "Yes, it is. But not always better." He directed the horse to where the black woman had pointed and said as he reined up at the last small shanty, "Do you want me to go with you?"

"Well . . ." Landra was exasperated at her ambivalence; she wasn't used to not knowing her own mind.

"I'll come." He tied the reins, and swung her down easily from the carriage, then escorted her to the little house. "Denis is right, you do need someone to look after you."

Landra frowned at him slightly as she knocked on the rough plank door. "He told you that, did he?"

Before he could answer, an old man opened the door, an astonished look on his face.

Sam'l was dumbfounded at the sight of the doctor and a pretty young white woman at his door, and when he realized who Landra was, he was moved almost to tears. He finally accepted the fact that they wanted to come inside and talk to him. He was small man, his face below the snow-white hair a maze of deep wrinkles, his mouth completely toothless. But that mouth never ceased to smile delightedly after he found she was the daughter of Marie D'Arcy, all grown-up and beautiful.

When Landra asked about the letters, the smile faded. "I'm awful glad you come, Mis' Landra," Sam'l said without looking at her. "But I got some stuff I gotta do now."

"But the letters—what about the letters, Sam'l?" Landra's distress was painfully obvious. Who else was there to ask?

"I druther not talk about it," the old man muttered, his hands moving again and again over the fringe of his white hair.

"But why?" Landra persisted. "Did someone tell you you mustn't?"

Sam'l stopped the movement of his hands and stared at her. "How you know that? She said she didn't tell no one—"

"Bethany! Why would she tell you such a thing?" In her anxiety Landra had, almost unknowingly, moved over to the old man and was grasping his arm.

Sam'l didn't speak for several tense moments, just stood staring at the slim white fingers that held tightly to the black skin of his arm. Then he whispered, "That's the way *she* done—held on so tight—and her so sick . . ."

Aware that she had probably been hurting him, Landra released the old man's arm and led him over to the one chair in the sparsely furnished, dim little room. She sat on the narrow bed frame that was covered with a patchwork quilt. "Please, Sam'l, tell me about my sister. I have to know, and there's no one but you to tell me."

In the long moments before he spoke, she smoothed the intricately stitched quilt. It was made in a pinwheel pattern, with spiky circles of bright rainbow colors. She remembered her mother beginning such a quilt; remembered the long lazy days outside when the women, white and black, worked together. Her mother had enjoyed quilting, even though it was unnecessary for her to do such things. Landra realized suddenly that this was very likely the same quilt.

"She—" Sam'l began, then, at Landra's sudden, agitated look, explained, "Miz Bethany called me in, up to her room, 'thout nobody else. That's whut she said, 'thout nobody else. She looked so pale, her face white as buttermilk. An' her voice—so soft I couldn't hardly hear." He stopped, and his rheumy old eyes filled with tears.

"Please go on, Sam'l," urged Landra. "What did she say?"

He drew a deep breath and glanced at Hollis, who was listening. Landra realized if he was ever going to say anything, it would be to her alone. "Dr. Freman, could you . . . would you mind waiting outside?"

"Are you sure?" he asked, his voice quiet, his face concerned.

She nodded, her eyes on the agitated old man. "If you don't mind, that is?"

"No, of course not, if that's what you want. I'll be just outside," he answered as he stepped through the door and closed it behind him.

Landra waited as patiently as she could. Finally, old Sam'l said, his voice quavering, "Miz Bethany, she tole me not to tell nobody—" He halted, and looked fearfully into the dim corners of the small room.

"But, Sam'l, surely she didn't mean me, the letters were for me! See, I have them here." She drew a small packet of envelopes from her bag and showed them to the old man, who began to tremble.

"She tole me she had six letters . . ." He watched as Landra pulled the satin ribbon from the letters and counted them. Sam'l nodded. "That's them. She say mail 'em one ever' month 'til they was gone. She said . . . said . . ." He wavered again.

"Yes, *what*? You can tell me!"

"She said keep all yore letters, and not give 'em to Dr. Adam; she didn't want him worried none." He went over to a little chest and got out several letters. "These is the ones that come from New York City. I kept 'em all."

Landra closed her eyes, ridiculously glad she'd been right in believing Adam had not known of her mother's death. But there was more she had to know. "Sam'l, was . . . was my sister very ill? When was the last time you saw her?" She could see the look of concentration on his face. "Was it six months ago, when she gave you the letters?"

He nodded, then frowned. "No'm, I guess it were longer than that, 'bout a month or so longer. She made me promise not to tell Dr. Adam, and I never seen her no more. He give me some money, though," he defended Adam quickly, and Landra was reminded of the young black woman's scathing remark earlier. There was one more question she had to ask, and it came slowly, painfully. "Sam'l, was Beth alive when you left the house?"

His cloudy old eyes rolled in fear; she could see his reluctance to speak. When he did, it was in an agonized whisper. "She was, but I knew she weren't long for this world. I was afraid if

I didn't do like she said, she'd . . . she'd come back and ha'nt me!"

Shocked, Landra said, "Did Bethany tell you that?"

"Oh, no'm, but . . ." He trailed off, clutching the small packet of Landra's own letters to Bethany.

"Sam'l, thank you. You've been a great help, and I appreciate it." She reached into her purse, found some money, and pressed it into his hand. "She would have wanted me to have my letters back, Sam'l. May I have them?"

For a moment he held them even tighter, his eyes searching the room as if looking for some ghostly, accusing figure. Then he gave them to Landra, who tucked them safely into her purse.

"Thank you, Sam'l," she repeated, "and God bless you. I'll come again, all right?"

But he had retreated from her, almost from reality. As she left, Landra could hear him muttering, "No'm, I won't tell nobody—*nobody*!" Perhaps he would even persuade himself he had told no one.

The bright sunlight made her squint, and Dr. Freman, his tone purposely light, said, "I've heard that southern ladies don't go out in midday, not if they don't want wrinkles and freckles."

She did not comment on his statement; absently, she allowed him to help her up into the carriage before she spoke. "It was good of you to bring me here. Thank you."

As the horse moved away form the old man's house he said, "Did you find the information you were looking for?"

"I suppose. It's all so confusing." From force of habit she pulled on her gloves; then, feeling the sticky heat of her hands, she pulled them off again.

He waited for her to speak, and when she didn't he was silent as well until they were almost in front of the Chaumont house. "I don't want to pry, please believe me. But I want you to know that if you need someone to talk to, just to give a sympathetic ear, I'm available."

Touched, she met his eyes. "I . . . I believe you really mean that."

"I do. You seemed so troubled when you came out."

She nodded, feeling the sting of tears. "I was. He told me some very disturbing things, things I can't quite sort out."

"Well, remember what I said, I'm here if you need me. You'd best go in; I think your admiration society is waiting for you." With a little smile he inclined his head to the Chaumont house where all three little girls, seated on the large porch swing, were waiting in obvious anticipation for Landra. As Dr. Freman assisted Landra from the carriage, the children hit the porch floor almost simultaneously and ran out to greet them.

"I had so wanted to stay at Greenlea," she said, almost to herself.

"I'm sure there's a logical explanation," said Dr. Freman, his concern plain in his voice and on his face. "Don't forget, I'm not far away if you need me. All right?"

As she watched him get back into the buggy, Landra said, "All right. And . . . thank you again, for everything."

"Why, miss, I haven't done anything yet," he said, his voice teasing now. "But if you give me half a chance, I'll move the state of Louisiana over an inch or two if that would help."

Landra laughed in spite of herself. "I almost believe you could!"

He gave a little wave and drove away. When he was gone, Landra felt heavyhearted again. Everything seemed so . . . so grim, and confusing. Adam had simply not wanted her at Greenlea, and Bethany . . . Bethany was not there. In the deepest corner of her mind, she knew where her gentle, beautiful sister was. But she wouldn't think about that, not now.

CHAPTER 4

Gratefully, Landra accepted the light lunch Mrs. Chaumont had prepared and afterward gave in to the older woman's insistence that she rest.

"Our climate is a lot different than you've been accustomed to. And you look as though you've had a hard morning already," Mrs. Chaumont said as she turned the bed down.

Landra was almost asleep when she heard the door open and saw Jeannette's pert, anxious face peer around it. " 'Scuse me, but could I just get my shoes, ma'am? I got to go over to Mimi's and pick blackberries—"

"Jeannette!" Her mother's voice rang out. "You bothering Miss Landra? Come on out of there, right now." She appeared beside Jeannette, and said apologetically, "I'm sorry, Landra. Child," she said, shaking her head at Jeannette, "you know better."

"But my shoes, I need my shoes. There's lots of rocks at Mimi's and you said wear my shoes when I went over there—" She darted into the room, reached under the bed, and with a sweet smile, directed first at Landra then at her mother, fled from the room.

Mrs. Chaumont started once more to apologize. "Children. A blessing and a burden."

After a short silence Landra said, "But this is her room, isn't it, Mrs. Chaumont? I'm imposing on you."

"Nonsense. As long as you need a place, we'd be proud to have you stay, Jeannette especially. She doesn't mind sleeping with the other girls a bit." She started to pull the door shut, then, in just the same tone she might have used to Jeannette, added, "You rest now, you hear?"

44

Surprisingly enough, Landra did rest. It was late afternoon when she woke, somewhat refreshed. Some time during the course of the afternoon she had reaffirmed her decision to find Bethany, regardless of what Adam said. As to her going back to New York . . . She found water in the blue pitcher and poured it out into the matching bowl in such an angry rush that it spilled. The water cooled her skin as she washed, but not the heated argument in mind.

Adam had treated her the same way he had five years before, as though she were a child. Well, there was surely some way to find out what was going on at Greenlea. It seemed that Adam thought she couldn't be trusted with the truth. She stopped suddenly; in a way, he was justified. Everyone was always saying, "Landra's one of those people who rush in where angels fear to tread. . . ." She sighed. Her prayers never failed to include a plea for patience. Then a wry smile played about her mouth as she thought, "God probably gets weary of me saying, 'Lord, give me patience, *right now*!' "

But she'd show Adam. Somehow, she'd carefully, discreetly find out the truth and show him by her calm, decisive actions that she was different. She dressed, thinking, as the black silk rustled on, that it was inevitable the last five years and the long, lingering illness of her mother had changed her. If Adam had given her a chance he'd have noticed, but he hadn't. With a yank she finished buttoning the bodice of her dress and went to find Mrs. Chaumont.

She found her in the kitchen, led by the smell of something cooking that made her mouth water. All three little girls were there, giggling frequently, stealing many admiring glances at Landra. "Something smells absolutely marvelous," she said. "What is it?"

"Gumbo," was the smiling reply her hostess gave as she took a clean spoon from the drawer, carefully scooped a spoonful from the round black pot on the stove, and offered it to Landra. "Taste?"

Landra sipped delicately at the fragrant broth. "Oh, that's really good! How do you make it?"

A fresh spate of giggles burst from the girls; then Jeannette said with a sidelong look at her mother, "Well, first you make a roux—" It was quite obvious she was mimicking her mama, who took it good-naturedly.

Rene Chaumont flipped her dish towel in mock anger at

Jeannette, then began to dish hot, fluffy rice into bowls. The girls efficiently set the bowls in the proper places on the table. "She's right, the little scamp. First you make a roux. Sit down, Landra, and we'll have supper."

Finding she was ravenously hungry, Landra did as she was bidden and made quick work of the delicious soup Rene ladled over the rice in her bowl. She said, "I'm afraid I'm making a pig of myself, but I've never eaten anything so good in all my life. What exactly is a roux, anyway? Is that what makes this taste so good?"

Rene nodded. "You bet. A roux is just flour and shortening, and you mix 'em up, then brown slow, slow, until it's the color of oh, say good caramel, or weak coffee, which you won't see too often hereabouts," she added slyly. She was rewarded by a smile from Landra. "Didn't you ever have Cajun cooking before?"

Landra shook her head. "Not that I can remember, and I would have remembered. Is it like Creole?"

"Sure, only it's different. Cajun cooking will make your tongue go crazy just to smell it. Take this, it's got crawfish in it, sort of poor man's lobster. Jeannette, why don't you tell Miss Landra about how crawfish got way down here in bayou country, anyhow?"

Jeannette tried hard to look modest, but she soon lost any self-consciousness as she warmed to her tale. "My papa, he was a Cajun; you know, like the Acadians that were run out of Nova Scotia way back in the 1700s?" She looked at Landra, who nodded encouragingly. "Anyway, they say the lobsters were left up there to make the trip by land by themselves. They had to walk, and the longer they walked, the littler they got. And by the time they got down here to the Atchafalaya, they was all shrunk down to crawfish size!"

Landra laughed, delighted. "What a marvelous story, Jeannette! And that old crawfish may be small, but he's sure tasty. If I could have just a little more . . ." She held out her bowl to Rene, who filled it with the pleased expression of a good cook whose labor is appreciated. "You'll have to teach me to make that roux."

The second girl, Jolie, piped up then. "Mama says that if a child do something bad and stop the cook and she burn the roux, that child gets two spankings—one for what he did, and one for making her burn the roux!"

"Hmm," said Landra, "I'll wager you don't often interrupt the cook."

The child shook her head vigorously. "Oh, no, ma'am!"

Joy, the baby, joined in, "Oh, no!"

Again Landra found herself laughing, and wondered briefly how she could in the face of the circumstances of the day. She only knew this simple, happy little family had faced trouble, and pain, and they could laugh; she accepted it and was humbly grateful for their warmth and hospitality. After a dish of blackberry cobbler with fresh cream, she sighed and said, "I'll be two hundred pounds if I keep this up."

Rene shrugged her shoulders and cautioned the trio to make sure the dishes were clean, dried, and put away before they left the kitchen. She poured small cups of very black coffee for herself and Landra from a battered old drip pot and suggested they sit outside on the swing on the front porch.

"It's cooler out here sometimes," she said, and gently started it swinging with her foot. The air was still quite warm, fragrant with honeysuckle and the heavier scent of the cape jasmine bush planted near the corner of the house. Landra took a sip of the coffee and couldn't keep a little grimace from her face. "Too strong, huh?" Rene asked, nodding knowingly. "Most folks don't care for Louisiana coffee if they weren't raised on it."

"My mother never let us girls have coffee," said Landra absently. "It's fine, really it is." She tried another taste, and put it down, an apologetic smile on her face. "Oh, I'm just—"

"You're worried about your sister," supplied Rene quietly. "I don't blame you."

"It's all so confusing, and no one can, or maybe no one will, tell me anything."

"I know. I wish there was some way I could help."

"Oh, you've helped more than I had any right to expect," said Landra quickly. "I hate to ask, but are you absolutely sure you can't think of anyone else I could talk to?"

The older woman frowned. "I would have said old Doc Freman, except that I understand he's pretty bad off. The young doctor isn't likely to have much information; he's only been in town a short while." Suddenly she gave a little exclamation. "Oh, I forgot, he was here."

"Dr. Freman?" said Landra, a pleased little feeling surprising her. "When? What did he want—" She halted, embarrassed at her eagerness.

Rene barely hid her amusement. "While you were napping. He said he wanted to make sure your head was all right, but I got the feeling he just wanted to see you."

Landra lowered her eyes. "Did he say he . . . whether or not he'd be—"

"Back?" Rene laughed outright. "Yes, he did! As a matter of fact if you'll look, yonder he comes."

Landra was amazed and somewhat chagrined at the surge of gladness she felt at the sight of Hollis Freman's tall, lean figure striding purposefully toward them. Had it really only been yesterday that she'd met him? The vagrant thought that plagued her each time she saw him came again; why did he seem so familiar? She smiled as he came up the steps. "Mrs. Chaumont tells me you came this afternoon to check on me. I . . . thank you; I appreciate it."

He stood with his back to the porch railing, his broad shoulders outlined against the dusky sky. "I'd like to take credit for being wonderfully conscientious, but the plain truth of the matter is, with only one patient it isn't too difficult." He laughed easily at himself, a nice sound indeed in the still, warm air.

Rene Chaumont rose from the swing. "Would you like some coffee? We were just having a cup."

"No, no thank you," he said. "What I actually came for was to see if Landra—Miss Cole—felt up to a walk. If I'm to build up a reputation as a conscientious physician, I should take a look at the dressing on her head, you understand, and it would be far easier in my grandfather's—ah, *my* office. Hard to get used to the idea."

Mrs. Chaumont nodded, a smile lurking at the corners of her mouth. "I understand. You feel up to it, don't you, Landra?" she asked, as though there was a doubt.

"Yes. As a matter of fact, a walk sounds nice." She got up and took the arm Hollis Freman offered. "I won't be long, Mrs. Chaumont."

"And Mrs. Olsen's at the house standing guard as usual," he said with a chuckle. As they moved toward the road, he called back, "You mustn't worry at all, Mrs. Chaumont; she's safe with me."

Walking quietly side by side in the gathering dusk, Landra thought with a bewilderingly deep sense of contentment that she did, indeed, feel safe with this man. Safe, and, though it seemed ambiguous, unsettled at the same time. "Dr. Freman—"

"Call me Hollis."

"But I hardly know you."

"That's not so. We're longtime acquaintances," he said, patting the hand that lay in the crook of his arm. "My memory is just better than yours."

She stopped, and he looked down into her puzzled face. "I did think . . . I felt I knew you, but I just couldn't figure out how," she said, her eyes searching his clean-lined face, the laughing blue eyes. He turned and began to walk again, and Landra was glad she was able to keep up with him easily.

"It has to do with a dead fish." His tone was solemn.

"A dead fish?"

"Uh-hum. And a group of very happy people."

They were nearing the neat white two-story house, and Landra saw that already the lights were on; a mometary pang shot through her as she thought of the dark windows at Greenlea. With an effort she said brightly, "Surely they weren't happy about the dead fish?"

"No, they were happy about—and with—me." He stopped on the porch, and his eyes had a faraway remembering look in them. "It was the happiest day of my life, the day I was baptized. That very morning I discovered that all those sermons I'd suffered through every Sunday, every summer, really meant something to me personally." His voice got a little quieter. "I discovered that Jesus loved *me*, that He died for *me*, and the whole thing was real, not just stories. I've never been the same since, praise God."

Landra's eyes were wide. "I do remember! The baptism was in the river, and we were all on the bank watching. How we laughed, the other children and me, and the grown-ups shushed us and tried to keep from giggling themselves when that huge old gar—it must have been five feet long—floated by!"

"Just as Pastor said, '. . . dead to your sins . . .' and laid me back, that thing went sailing by in the current. When I came up wanting to shout because I was so happy, there you all were, laughing to beat the band. I thought you were pleased with me. Then I saw that thing, belly-up and way past his prime."

"We were, pleased with you, I mean. Your face was so . . . it was almost shining," she said, a little wistful now at the memory. She also remembered thinking that young Hollis had had an experience she envied for some reason she couldn't fathom at the time, for she had been baptized the summer before. "There's something else I remember about you now."

"What's that?" He was standing fairly close and his blue eyes held hers.

"Your ears used to stick out," she said. "They don't now," she added, thinking they were very nice ears.

He laughed delightedly, head thrown back. "Well, thank the Lord, my head grew out to meet them or they flattened themselves, or something. I remember very well how you looked."

Landra shivered at the sudden low intensity of his words. She tried to speak lightly. "Oh? Do you remember that I had more freckles than Carter has Liver Pills?"

The light of day had all but faded away; Hollis Freman leaned even closer, his eyes warm and steady. "I can't see any now . . . your face is . . ."

Landra wasn't even aware she was holding her breath, and it came out in a little rush when she heard someone behind them say quite loudly, "Well, I see you're back. Did you want me to serve tea after you've treated Miss Cole?"

"Oh, yes, of course, Mrs. Olsen. Come inside, Miss Cole, and I'll get things together." His voice was brisk and professional now, quite unlike that soft, almost intimate tone of a moment before.

Landra was quiet as she followed the two inside, her thoughts of that long ago day, of how . . . the only word to describe his face was radiant, perhaps joyous. She studied him covertly as he set out cotton wool, antiseptic, fresh bandages. Though his expression was serious now, she could still detect an underlying happiness, an enviable peace.

As he removed the bandage carefully, she heard him say with satisfaction, "Looks good. Wouldn't want a scar on that lovely forehead, would we?"

He had a new, smaller square of gauze on it before she could frame a reply; then Mrs. Olsen came bustling in. "Here's your tea!" she boomed. "Will you be wanting anything else?"

"No, no thank you, Mrs. Olsen," returned Hollis in a voice almost as loud as hers.

"Then I'll go up to my room." As she paused at the bottom of the mahogany staircase, she said, "But I'll be right upstairs if you need me." She gave Landra a meaningful look, then turned.

They both watched her march up the stairs, then Landra almost exploded with repressed laughter. "Doctor, I do believe she thinks I may be after you!" It was wonderful to feel gay, and carefree, and . . . young again. Landra realized how very difficult the past years had been for her.

When he'd gotten his own laughter under control, he caught her eyes with his steady gaze. "Any chance her suspicions are well founded?"

Gravely she answered, "Dr. Freman, you are as safe with me as you assured Mrs. Chaumont I am with you."

He grinned, then sighed. "Too bad." Then he said suddenly, "Well, take your tea, sit beside me here," he patted the ornate love seat, "and tell me exactly what's been going on."

"I . . . what do you mean?"

"You know what I mean. What happened at Greenlea last night, and why you wanted to go to Low Woods, what the old man told you that disturbed you so—everything." When she hesitated, her face a study of conflicting emotions, he said quietly, "Unless, of course, you feel as though you can't trust me yet."

"Oh, no, it's not that; I do trust you."

"Well, you need to tell someone, I can see that. It might as well be me."

So Landra took a deep breath, a long drink of the cold tea, and began. His blue eyes were so earnest and he gazed at her with such assurance, it seemed the most natural thing in the world to pour out the whole story, even to show him the puzzling letters. She felt an enormous relief in having told someone.

"Hmm." He rubbed the dent in his chin with the knuckle of his forefinger. "First, we must find out if your sister is alive, and if so, where she is. Then we must decide on the best course of action. Do you agree?"

His words were so direct they would have been cruel if not for the very real concern behind them. She nodded, unable to speak for a moment. Then she said slowly, "I . . . I wish I could say I haven't thought of the possibility that she's dead. But it's all so strange. The letters—why would she have written such meaningless letters?"

He shook his head. "I don't know. The thing that is so puzzling to me is your brother-in-law's behavior. From what little my grandfather said, he's a good man, a man of the utmost integrity."

"Something has happened; I know it." Landra felt the tightness in her throat, knew tears were not far behind. She wasn't the kind to cry easily. "I just don't know what to do, how to go about finding out the truth. If only Adam hadn't refused to allow me to stay at Greenlea. If only . . ." She squeezed her eyes shut and put a trembling hand over them.

For a moment Hollis Freman sat still, struck like most men by the sight of a woman's threatened tears. Then he moved closer and put a hand on her shoulder. "Don't, please don't. Look, I've told you I have plenty of time. I'll help you, and together we'll get to the bottom of all this. I'll ask around; and whatever else you can think of, just let me know. You're not alone, Landra."

His hand was warm and firmly comforting on her shoulder. "I can't tell you how much better those words make me feel," she said softly. "I suppose it's because that's exactly how I've been feeling—alone—since last night when the house was so dark, and I saw . . . that man."

"That's another thing. It's too bad you didn't get a better look at him. In that dim light you could have imagined a lot of things." Seeing her expression he hastily added, "I don't mean you imagined it at all. I just meant neither you nor I know exactly what you saw. And we need to know. How's this: tomorrow morning I'll pick you up at Chaumont's, and we'll ride out to Greenlea and take a look at things. You do ride horseback, don't you?" She nodded. "Good. Until then we'll just have to trust that God has His hand in all this, and that He'll guide us."

He was so sure, so vibrantly positive that Landra felt a little stab of envy, a longing to have such assurance. "Yes," she said faintly, "you're right. God will guide us."

"And now I'd better get you home . . . or to the Chaumont's, I mean." He smiled, and that lock of fair hair dangled over his eye. "They've taken quite an interest in you, and have been no small help, I gather."

That fact was one Landra agreed with fervently, and a bit later Hollis, as he'd insisted again that she call him, left her at the Chaumont house with a reminder that he would call for her at nine the next morning. It had been a strange evening, thought Landra as she slowly dressed for bed in the silent, dark house. Hollis Freman was no ordinary young man. She turned back the covers and lay down, her eyes accustomed now to the darkness. There was a sliver of a moon low in the sky outside, and the temperature had dropped a degree or two, at least enough to make sleep possible.

But she did not sleep. The conversation with Hollis about Bethany and the grave possibilities made her wide awake. Where was she? Was she alive? If she was, why was Adam so disturbed? Why had he been so evasive? The questions buzzed like angry bees in her mind. She tried to pray, to ask for that assurance that came to Hollis so easily. But it didn't come. All that consumed her tortured mind was fear for her sister and resentment against Adam, against the whole awful situation. Sleep was long in coming for Landra Cole that night.

CHAPTER 5

It had been no easy thing to escape the inquisitive, proprie-
tary Chaumont family. The horses they rode were walking con-
tentedly side by side down the road which led to Greenlea. Hollis Freman laughed. "Young Chaumont acted more like your
father than someone several years your junior! After that lec-
ture about staying out too late last night, I'm surprised he let
you come with me," he teased.

Landra responded quickly, defending Denis, "He's had to be
the man of his family for over two years now since his father
drowned. I think he's very mature and responsible for a sixteen-
year-old. He's certainly been helpful to me."

She met his eyes as he turned their clear blue gaze on her
and said, "I'm glad he took care of you, at least until you met
me."

Instead of being pleased at such a statement, Landra was
irritated. She kicked her horse and it sprang forward. Over her
shoulder she called back to the startled young man, "You're all
alike! What makes you think every woman is longing to be
taken care of? Some of us can manage just fine without you!"

Before he could catch up to her, Landra had reached the
curving drive which led to Greenlea. She stopped in the shade
of a huge old magnolia tree and waited quietly until Hollis
galloped up.

He studied her for a moment before he spoke. "Landra, I'm
sorry if I offended you in some way. I honestly didn't mean—I
don't really know what—"

He was so earnest Landra was instantly contrite. "Oh, Hollis, I'm the one who should apologize. I don't know why I blurt
out things like that. It wasn't even what I really feel, or meant
to say."

"It's all right, Landra," he soothed.

Quite suddenly she had an overwhelming need to clarify the situation, to *know* what she felt and wanted to say, and further, to understand the young man before her. "No, Hollis, it isn't all right. People—*I*—shouldn't blurt things out, especially when it . . . when it matters. It's just that men tend to think all women are helpless, when a lot of times the opposite is true."

He nodded slowly, his eyes holding hers. "You're right, of course. Women have strengths we men either know nothing about or, for very obscure reasons indeed, choose to ignore."

"And it seems to me if we could—men and women, I mean— find out more about each other, we could share things better." Hesitantly, hopefully, she searched his face for some sign that he understood, perhaps even agreed with her. She had certainly never heard a man, or even a woman, for that matter, voice such ideas. But she knew in her heart there was truth in them. She also knew it was ridiculously important that Hollis Freman acknowledge this.

He didn't disappoint her. Softly he said, "What you're talking about is a partnership, Landra. A man and a woman sharing both joys and burdens. Am I right?"

She nodded, not trusting herself to speak for a moment, feeling emotions that threatened to overcome her. She was aware that she'd never met a man like Hollis Freman, and it was quite possible she wouldn't again. She turned away, unable to sort out her feelings, and looked down the drive toward the house. From this distance, even in the bright morning sunlight, the decay was not apparent. It was a lovely sight, with its tall, graceful columns and matching chimneys.

"Are you ready to go now?" Hollis indicated the house with a nod of his head. "I promise to make my watchcare over you as inoffensive as I can."

It was impossible not to respond to his smile, the little crinkles at the corner of his eyes. She shook her head. "No, not yet. Let's ride for a while, maybe toward the river. I don't think I'm ready to face—" She broke off, unwilling even to say Adam's name aloud. "Let's ride, all right?"

He nodded agreement, and they cantered away from Greenlea, their horses in step, like two people who walk together. The intervening years since she had seen this road had made even more of a difference than she'd noticed in the town the night before. Ten years is a long time, enough for trees to grow more than twice as tall as she remembered. There were pines, huge oaks and magnolias, sweetgums with their maple-like leaves, and a tangled profusion of undergrowth. It was like a leafy tunnel, vividly green, and much cooler than it had been in the bright sunlight. At the end of the road was the river, the mighty Mississippi. It was very broad here and looked sluggish and slow-moving.

But Landra was reminded of the countless times her father had warned them as children of the treachery of these waters. Beneath the muddy surface, the river was swift and dangerous, and had claimed untold lives of those who had misread it.

Hollis broke the silence, which up to now had been punctuated only by the occasional call of a pair of red-winged blackbirds. "That's quite a river," he said respectfully. "Say, we passed what looked like a drive awhile back. Is there another home nearby?"

"Yes, Elkhorn plantation. I don't believe anyone's lived in the house for quite some time, though."

"I'd like to see it. These old places fascinate me, with their amazing diversification of architectonics," he said seriously.

Landra couldn't help but laugh outright. "*What* is architectonics?"

Grinning, he said, "Nothing but structural design, or skill. But architectonics sounds a lot more sophisticated, don't you think?"

"I certainly do, but where did you dig up such a term?"

"My father is the exception to the rule that all Freman men become doctors. He's an architect, and quite a brilliant one, too. I chose to follow Grandfather Freman's example, but it didn't keep me from being fascinated by architecture."

"Well, I'd be happy to hear all about it," Landra said, amused at his earnestness. She reined her horse around, and Hollis followed suit as they went back through the cool, green tunnel, stopping as they glimpsed the Elkhorn plantation house through the trees. They dismounted and walked closer, still hidden by the trees. It was an imposing structure, much larger than Greenlea, fully three stories high.

"Would you look at that!" breathed Hollis. "It's chiefly designed along Romanesque lines, but there are quite a few Victorian details like those."

Landra listened as he described the ornate building: its steep-pitched roof above which rose high ornamental chimneys and minarets, the wings that projected to east and west, and the dormers on all sides. In front of the main entrance and around the circular corner bay, there was a very delicate wrought-iron grille, as well as additional wrought-iron balconies which protruded from the third story. He was very knowledgeable, and though she was anything but, it was nonetheless extremely interesting to hear him talk about the house that was only a distant dream from her early childhood.

Then she saw the two figures standing close together at the far end of the old mansion. Landra knew instantly who the man was, even with his back turned. That straight, uncompromising back, the black suit and blacker hair . . . but who was the woman?

She was facing them, and Landra could see clearly how beautiful she was. Hollis was looking upward, shading his eyes against the bright sun, expounding with enthusiasm about one of the minarets which evidently had some fascinating peculiarity of its own. The pair had not seen them, and Landra studied the woman's face carefully, noting the abundance of jet hair, her dark brows and eyes, the magnolia complexion. She was slender and petite, so much so that she was forced to bend her head far back to look up into Adam's face. She was speaking earnestly, from her expression, as though she were trying to persuade him about something.

It was her next gesture that made Landra gasp involuntarily. The woman reached up with her hands, which even from this distance Landra could see had surprisingly long, thin fingers. She placed them on either side of his face and drew him down to her until his cheek rested on hers. They stood thus, not touching except for their faces, until Landra could bear it no longer.

"Hollis!" she whispered, for she was afraid the pair, though seemingly engrossed in each other, would see them. Landra was sure they had not, yet. "Please, let's leave—"

Puzzled, Hollis glanced down at her, then caught sight of the man and woman. "Who—"

But Landra took his arm and pulled him away, back toward the horses. Frantically she told herself as they walked that perhaps it wasn't he, that it was someone else. But one last, unwilling glance told her she'd been right. The sight of Adam's Indian-straight nose and tightly closed, black-lashed eyes, his carved, compressed mouth so close to the woman's dark hair sent a shaft of pain through her body. As she hesitated, she saw a man come toward the two, a man Landra had never seen before. Adam drew away from the woman as the man joined them, talking and gesturing emphatically.

Hollis helped Landra onto her horse, then mounted his own. He sat for a moment, chewing his lip. Then he said slowly, a frown on his face, "Did you know any of them? It seems as though I've seen the second man somewhere, the one who came out of the house."

"I don't know him, or *her*," Landra answered, ashamed of the angry tears which she tried to squeeze back.

"Hey, now," said Hollis sympathetically, and reached over to take her hand. "Come on, tell me what's hit you so hard. Who is that other man?"

She slapped her horse with the reins and trotted away. Puzzled, Hollis kicked his mount and rode up even with her. He didn't speak again, but rode beside her in silence. Finally his quietness, his acceptance of her stormy mood, had its effect. She calmed down enough to begin haltingly, "It was Adam, Dr. Jarret. My sister's husband." He nodded encouragingly. "I don't know the woman. But Adam always was attractive to women—"

Landra choked, and her hands came up involuntarily to her throat. The reins slipped down, but the gentle, obedient horse merely came to a halt and stood with his head lowered. Hollis leaped from his saddle and came around, reaching up to help Landra dismount. His arm across her shoulders, he led her to the shade of a gnarled, wide-spreading old oak tree. It was heavily hung with droopy, gray Spanish moss, almost reaching the soft, green carpet of grass below. They sat down, and again Hollis waited until she was calm. "All right, you obviously believe that those two were having some kind of secret tryst, that it's behind your sister's back, and he's involved with that woman."

"Hollis, do you have to state things so baldly?" Landra wailed.

"I'm sorry; I guess it's a habit I picked up in medical school." He patted her hand and smiled apologetically. "Your sister doesn't look anything like that woman, I take it? You couldn't have been mistaken?"

Landra took a deep breath. "My sister has hair like spun gold, as I've heard admiring young men say often enough, and she is—was—as tall as I am . . ."

He looked at her steadily. "Why do you say *was*?"

"Because I have a feeling . . . I've had it since the day before yesterday, when I first went to Greenlea."

"A feeling?"

It was a minute before Landra could answer, her voice scarcely more than a whisper. "Yes. My sister is dead. I *know* it; don't ask me how. And when I saw him with that woman I couldn't bear it—"

He slipped a comforting arm around her shoulders and squeezed lightly. "All right. Let's decide on the best course of action."

"That's what you said last night," Landra said, her tone implying, *And look where it got us*. She stiffened suddenly.

"I know exactly what I'm going to do. I'm going to move into *my home*"—she emphasized the last two words—"and find out what happened to Bethany."

"But I thought Dr. Jarrett refused to allow you to stay," Hollis said.

"Dr. Jarrett is busy at the moment," Landra answered bitterly. "If we hurry, we can get my things and I can get into the house before he returns."

"I don't think that's very wise, Landra. There must be another way to go about this thing."

Landra got to her feet, brushed furiously at the skirt of her riding habit, and walked away from the young man who stood frowning after her. She stood by her horse and said, "Are you going to help me up, or shall I get on alone? I can, you know, and I can move into Greenlea without your help, too. It would be harder, but I can."

He hurried over and helped her mount. "Don't be angry with me, Landra. It's just that I think it would be better if you—"

"I'm perfectly capable of deciding for myself what's better for me. Will you help me, or not?"

He stared up at her for a long minute, at the defiant, brilliant green eyes, the firmly set, lovely mouth, and concluded that she meant what she said. He shook his head. "You're stubborn. Did anyone ever tell you that?"

She melted a little and answered ruefully, "At least twice a day. Please, Hollis, I have to do it, and . . . and I do need someone. Will you help me?"

He chuckled and swung onto his horse. "I would have helped you when you were nasty. You can believe I will when you ask so prettily."

Mrs. Chaumont was most unwilling to let Landra go when they went for her things. She kept saying she was so sorry Jeannette had made her unwelcome, that they wanted her to feel free to stay as long as she liked.

But Landra was firm. "Greenlea is home, Mrs. Chaumont, and there's nowhere else in the world I belong now. It isn't that Jeannette made me feel unwelcome. Far from it," she said, smiling at the sweet-faced little girl who was watching anxiously. "Jeannette and I are friends, and I intend to come back and visit her often, so we can read together, like she and . . . Bethany did. All right, Jeannette?"

This was apparently more than all right with Jeannette, for she nodded furiously, still unable to speak. *How terrible*, she was thinking, *that Miss Landra might think I didn't want her!*

Landra put her arm around Mrs. Chaumont. "Tell Denis where I've gone, and not to worry. Denis is as great a worrier as you are. Besides, Dr. Freman has appointed himself my official watchdog." She turned to go, then asked slowly, "Mrs. Chaumont, do you know a strikingly pretty young woman with very black hair, a small woman, probably several inches shorter than I, who might be a—a friend of Dr. Jarrett's?"

Her eyes met those of the older woman who gave a long, almost painful sigh. She nodded. "Yes, I think so. It sounds like Carrie."

"Who is she?" Landra asked reluctantly. She wasn't sure she wanted to know.

"It's kind of complicated. She's a Chaumont, worse luck. But you know how these things are; she's the daughter of my husband's brother's first wife—that kind of thing. Some are in-laws, some are out-laws." She smoothed the soft brown hair from her forehead. "Carrie is not exactly an out-law, but she's not a good girl, either, not like I want my girls to be." She looked with pride at her daughters.

"You mean she's a—"

Quickly Mrs. Chaumont interrupted. "I'm not being fair. It could be that a lot of the things they say about her aren't true. But then . . . there's the baby—" She stopped, indecision plain on her face. When she spoke again it was not of a baby. "All I know is she's the kind that turns men's heads."

"She has a baby?" Landra asked. Mrs. Chaumont nodded but didn't speak. "And she isn't married. That's it, isn't it?"

"Yes." Her obvious reluctance to say anything further kept

Landra from asking any more questions. As she watched Landra open the door to leave, however, she added, "If you need someone, will you remember I'm here?"

"Yes, of course. Thank you for all you've done." She gave her hand to Mrs. Chaumont, who pressed it warmly.

Once more they loaded Landra's things into a carriage, and after Hollis had stopped off at his grandfather's house, he climbed back in and said, "There was something I wanted to get. Do you need to go anywhere else?"

She started to say no, but a thought that had been floating in and out of her mind finally lodged itself firmly. "Yes, I'd like to go to the Catholic church, if you don't mind."

"Not at all," he said, and if he was curious, he didn't voice it. The church was at the opposite end of town from old Dr. Freman's house, and he tied the horse at the iron railing that bordered the churchyard. Just as they were about to enter, Landra caught sight of a large, ornate headstone at the corner of the cemetery at the rear of the church. Impulsively she walked back to it, and made a quick, systematic search of the names carved on the stones. As is common in marshy country, the dead were buried above ground, making the small graveyard look very cluttered. Landrum Cole had insisted he be buried in his native New York, and Marie Cole's last request to her daughter had been that she lie beside her husband, even if it meant she would never return to Louisiana.

Landra released a small, pent-up explosion of breath. "There are no Coles here, Hollis, and no Jarretts, either."

He had come up behind her, and stood waiting quietly. "Did you expect there would be?"

"I don't know . . . I don't know what I expected!" When he didn't speak she turned, contrite again. "I'm sorry, Hollis. None of this is your fault, and yet I seem to be taking my frustration out on you."

He took her hand and tucked it into the crook of his arm. "If that's the only way I can help, then hammer away. But I really think we should be going."

"No, not yet. I want to see the priest, Father Etienne. Denis told me about him."

By now Hollis recognized the determined tone in her voice, and silently accompanied her into the church. He sat alone in the back of the small frame building while she followed the old priest to his study. The building itself might have been modest, but the stained-glass windows were nothing short of spectacular with the bright summer sun streaming through. Landra noticed only dimly the noble saints and the depictions of the slaying of certain horrendous dragons; the explosion of color in each of the treasured windows was wasted on her. It was bright in the sanctuary, and when she entered Father Etienne's study, the cool dimness was welcome. She sat in the chair he pointed to.

Having introduced herself when they had entered the church, Landra was, for a moment, at a loss as to how to begin. Father Etienne sat silently, his dark blue eyes intent, watching. His expression was one of polite interest; there was nothing else, no hint of recognition past that flicker she'd sensed at their initial meeting. Even as a young girl growing up at Greenlea, she had worshiped exclusively at the small, infinitely plain church at the other end of town. Its people had had a reputation for plainness as well, in the simple order of service and lack of hierarchy in their clergy. But she felt, purely from an intuitive sense, that Father Etienne was a reasonable, fair-minded man. Still, when she finally gathered courage to speak, her words were so subdued that the man had to lean forward slightly to hear them.

"Father Etienne, I . . . I've come to ask about my . . . sister Bethany, Mrs. Adam Jarrett. Surely you know her."

He hesitated and Landra felt, rather than actually saw, his withdrawal. His voiced guarded, carefully neutral, he said, "Yes, of course."

"What's happened to her? No one can, or will, tell me. How long has it been since she came to services, to confession?"

He was silent for so long that Landra was about to insist he answer her. But then he said, "Mrs. Jarrett was not able to attend services last year because of her health. I went often to Greenlea to hear her confession, and to be of what small comfort I could."

"What was wrong with Bethany?"

The directness of Landra's question made the priest draw a sharp little breath. Then he sighed and said, "I am not at liberty to divulge that information. Surely you can understand—it was a privileged communication between a confessor and her priest."

"Doesn't the fact that I am her sister make any difference? Please, you must tell me—was my sister alive the last time you saw her?"

After another moment's hesitation, Father Etienne drew a deep breath and answered, "Yes, I heard her confession and administered the last rights, because she was very near death. But I was called away, and she was still alive when I saw her last."

"But she's dead now, isn't she, Father?" Landra waited, but the priest did not answer this time. "I looked for her grave outside, but she isn't there." In an anguished whisper she said, "Why, Father Etienne? If she's dead, why isn't she buried in the churchyard?"

"Miss Cole, you are asking questions I cannot answer. I am bound by the laws of the church; I cannot break them. And there are other factors involved which make it impossible for me to help you. I'm very sorry."

"But Father—"

His eyes were filled with sympathy, but he only shook his head; she knew he would not, could not, tell her more. She felt a terrible weight of helplessness settle over her. Was there no one who would answer her questions, who would give an honest answer?

Father Etienne rose and went to the door, opening it wide for Landra. There was nothing she could do but leave, for he obviously was unwilling to talk any further. She walked slowly back to where Hollis waited, and was grateful when he did not question her. She badly needed the easy silence he provided on the drive to Greenlea. As they approached the house, however, Landra grew more and more apprehensive.

What if Adam were there? Worse yet, what if he had brought *her* there? Landra could even imagine her opening the door. . . .

CHAPTER 6

But it was not the beautiful black-haired woman who opened the door at Greenlea. It was a small, pale girl who looked two or three years younger than Landra, even though her brown hair was drawn back severely from her face and fastened in a tight, matronly knot. She stared at Landra and Dr. Freman nervously, her light blue eyes anxious, then said, "Yes, may I help you?"

Landra got the impression that helping them was the last thing the girl wanted to do, that she'd much prefer closing the door immediately in their faces. She glanced back into the house several times as Landra answered, "I'm Landra Cole, Mrs. Jarrett's sister, and I . . . I'm here to—" Suddenly Landra was very angry. Why should she have to go through all this again? Without touching the girl she slipped by her into the house. "Come on in, Dr. Freman," she said, hoping the fact that Hollis was a doctor would make a difference.

It made a difference, all right. With one horrified look at him, the girl slammed the door in his face. "What are you doing?" Landra cried.

The girl's eyes were wide with fear. "It's bad enough you're in—but if you're really Mrs. Jarrett's sister—"

"I am! But why did you shut Dr. Freman out?"

"He wouldn't stand for another doctor being here when he's gone. I've heard them talk, him and Dr. Delacroix, about the other doctors, and they don't want them to know—"

Landra was suddenly, inexplicably frightened. What did Adam have to hide? Just as she started to phrase the question, Hollis began to knock loudly on the door. "Landra?" she heard him call.

64

For one long, indecisive moment Landra looked from the door to the girl standing beside her, whose pale face seemed even paler in the semi-darkness of the entryway. "Look, what is your name?"

"Rose," she whispered.

"Rose, if you'll just let Dr. Freman bring my things in and give me a moment to explain what's happening, I promise he'll leave right away and come back when Dr. Jarrett can be here to meet him. All right?" She spoke softly, trying to calm the girl. "We won't let him past the hall, I promise. I'm afraid if we don't he won't go away; he'll be too concerned for me. You see that, don't you?" Rose nodded, but still made no move to open the door. It was Landra who let Hollis in, his face drawn and anxious.

"What's going on?" He practically sputtered the words.

"It's all right, Hollis," Landra soothed. "Just leave my things here, and you can come back later and meet my brother-in-law."

"But, Landra, are you sure that's what you want?" He had come to stand close beside her, his eyes dark with concern. "I really don't want to leave you here like this. It's worse than I thought."

Landra put a hand on his arm and was amazed at how much comfort that simple contact gave. "I don't see any other way, Hollis. Adam left very strict, very specific orders for Rose, and I'm afraid he'll be angry when he finds me here. If you were here as well, it would be worse for her. You understand, don't you?" she pleaded. She wasn't happy about his leaving, but she felt it was necessary.

He sighed deeply. "I can't pretend I like this. How will you get word to me if you need something?"

Suddenly it was as though she and Hollis were quite alone; Landra swallowed hard as she gazed up into his eyes. "I'll get word to you . . . the important thing is that you'll be there. I . . ." How could she say what she was thinking, that she couldn't imagine when she hadn't had him to rely on? It seemed as though he had always been there. She reached up and touched his smooth cheek lightly; her breath caught lightly at the scent of the aftershave he wore. He smelled so clean, so fresh. "It won't be long." She didn't say until what; somehow Landra felt they both knew that she simply meant it wouldn't be long before they saw each other again, for whatever reason.

Then he was gone, leaving Landra to smile nervously at Rose. "I think I'll take my old room if that's all right. Will you help me carry these up?"

Rose nodded solemnly and together they soon had Landra settled in the small bedroom that faced the front of the house. The pale, slight girl stood uncertainly in the doorway. "He won't like it, you know. He'll be angry with me for letting you in."

"Dr. Jarrett?" Rose nodded, her blue eyes frightened. Landra took a deep breath. "Well, you leave him to me. When do you expect him home?"

Rose hunched her shoulders. "We never know. Look, I do the cooking. If you'll stay here and not come down, I'll bring your dinner up. I'll tell him you're here."

Landra sympathized with the misery in the girl's expression, but she felt she couldn't make such a promise. Aloud she said, "Don't worry, Rose, everything will be all right."

Rose shook her head slowly. "No, that's not true." She slipped out of the room, leaving Landra alone.

Unwilling somehow to unpack her things, Landra wandered about the small room. The oak bureau was the same, but its deep drawers held none of the familiar scent of lavender that had been there when her mother was alive and lady of the house. This house had no lady, now; she was dead, and buried—but not in the churchyard. For a woman like Bethany to be refused burial in hallowed ground had such terrible implications that Landra could only wring her hands at the thought, wondering why such a thing should be.

She waited, not patiently, for almost an hour before she went out into the hall, telling herself she hadn't promised Rose, not really. The house was quiet, and all the bedroom doors were shut. The worn dark red carpet on the stairs absorbed any sound her feet made as she crept down them. At the foot she hesitated, glancing into the drawing room, but there was no one there, no sound. The kitchen her father had built was to the left, and Landra walked slowly down the hall toward it, noting that here, too, the doors were shut. It was as though the house was closed in upon itself.

As she neared the kitchen door, she heard voices: Rose's, she thought, and a man's. No, she decided as she got closer, it was two men. One she'd never heard before. And the other . . . She put her hand to her throat. It sounded like the man who'd been in the old kitchen that first night she came.

It wasn't bravery that prompted her to burst into the room; more likely it was that certain form of recklessness that has won more battles than real courage. The scene within printed itself indelibly on her brain. The kitchen was much as she remembered it, long and narrow with a correspondingly long and narrow trestle table her father had designed and had made especially to fit the room. The two men had obviously been seated at the table eating, and the one whose terrible voice Landra recognized jumped up, upsetting his bowl and glass. He put his arms up to shield his face and ran from the room, leaving the others in shocked silence. Rose stood by the old black stove, horror and accusation mingled in her expression as she whispered, "I asked you to stay upstairs. I thought you would . . ."

Landra started to say she was sorry, that she'd gotten tired of waiting, when her eyes met those of the young man seated at the table. There was not much light in the room, but even in the dimness Landra could see the dull red flush on his face, the unmistakable look of illness stamped on his boyish, good-looking features. He didn't speak; none of the three did for a long moment.

It was Rose who broke the spell. "Jimmy," she choked out, "Jimmy darling, you'd better go . . . please, you'd better go."

She came around the table, deliberately shielding the young man from Landra's view. She took his arm and started to lead him to the door, but he shook her off and said, "Don't! I'm not helpless yet!" But Landra could tell by the way he put out his hands as he stumbled that he was very nearly blind. He touched the door facing and went out, hands feeling along the wall as he walked toward what used to be Landra's father's study, now the laboratory.

His shuffling footsteps died away. In the brief silence that followed, Rose began picking up the scattered dishes, mopping up the spilled soup. When she spoke her voice was low and accusing. "You shouldn't have come down here. I asked you not to." She sank into the chair the young man had almost overturned, put her head on her arms, and, to Landra's extreme discomfort, began to sob bitterly. "Oh, Jimmy . . . Jimmy!"

Landra waited until Rose quieted somewhat, then said, "Is Jimmy your husband?"

This only provoked a fresh outburst of tears. Muffled though they were, Landra caught most of the words that poured out of the anguished girl. "No, and he'll never be! If only Dr. Adam could find . . ."

"If Dr. Adam could find what, Rose?" But nothing Landra said could induce Rose to say anything more. She was still trying to get the girl to talk when Lucas Delacroix came into the room.

"Miss Cole! What are *you* doing here?" His eyes took in the huddled form of Rose, and Landra's look of frustration.

Landra decided to bluff him. "I'm just checking on dinner, Dr. Delacroix. Rose is a little upset because I scolded her, but we'll work it out." She swept regally to the door, and called back to Rose, "There now, Rose, you'll soon get the way of it. I'm not all that difficult to please."

Lucas followed her as she walked swiftly into the drawing room and began to yank off the offensive dust covers. "What are you doing here?" he asked again.

She finished taking the sheets off the last piece of furniture, then drew the rose draperies back, letting the afternoon sun into the room. Even with the lovely furniture uncovered the room had a stale, unlived-in look. To the startled young man who stood staring at her Landra said, "You're repeating yourself, Doctor. As to your question, I'm trying to decide just what will have to be done to set this place right. This," she made a wide, sweeping gesture with her arm, "will require help from town. Rose and I can't possibly do it alone. As to the upstairs, I've not had time to see to it. I'll do it now."

Before he could reply she shoved the armload of sheets at him and was out of the room and halfway up the stairs. "Miss Cole—" Landra glanced back, only to see the amazed young doctor still holding the sheets. When he saw where she was headed, he dropped them and raced after her. But she already had the door to the master bedroom open.

"You mustn't go in there. Dr. Jarrett doesn't allow anyone in there!"

Landra didn't answer. She was being assailed by far too many sense impressions. The room was dim, but she could see the big, canopied bed, the heavy, ornately carved chests and blue damask draperies. It was the odor that repelled her, making her step backward, almost into the arms of Lucas Delacroix.

"What is that odor?" she whispered. It wasn't heavy or overpowering; in reality it was only a light, lingering ghost of itself. Landra knew she had never smelled it, or anything like it, before.

"I . . . I don't know what you mean," Lucas stammered. But he was totally unconvincing.

She started to question him again, but the sound of a door opening and closing below stopped her. Deep, angry tones mingled with Rose's lighter, breathless ones, and with a sinking heart Landra realized yet another person was getting a tongue-lashing because she had been allowed into the house. Quickly, without any conscious thought of why she was doing it, she stepped back into the room, walked over to a chair she remembered as a favorite of her mother's, and sat down.

She didn't have long to wait. Adam stormed into the room and came to stand over her, a tall, dark-faced, formidable stranger. With a sudden icy calmness she realized he was just that—a stranger. He hardly resembled the man who'd captured all their hearts so long ago in New York.

When he spoke his voice was low, but so full of anger that she shrank back against the soft velvet of the cusion. "You had to come back."

"Yes, I did," she said defiantly, if a trifle weakly.

"What am I going to do with you?"

She stared at him—the tight, compressed mouth, the fierce black eyes with all their ugly anger directed at her. Then she stood up, and though her heart hammered, demanded, "Tell me the truth. Tell me how Bethany died—when, and where she's buried, and why she isn't buried in the church ground."

When he still refused to speak, she drew the packet of letters from her purse and said, "Every month for the last six months I've received one of these." She riffled them out, like a deck of cards. "A month ago I wrote that Mother was dead, and this was the answer I got. But answer's not the right word. Read it."

He took the letter, opened it slowly, and read it. Landra knew he did; his eyes scanned the lines. But his expression never changed. "Mardi Gras?" His lips formed the words almost soundlessly.

She nodded wearily. "Yes. I write that her mother's dead, and get a letter back about how marvelous Mardi Gras is this year. That's when I decided to come . . . to see what . . ." She faltered, then explained how she'd visited old Sam'l, and of the promise Bethany had asked of him. When she repeated his words about how Bethany hadn't wanted "Dr. Adam to worry none," Adam put a hand to his eyes and stifled a groan.

"I didn't know she'd written those. If I had . . ." Landra was watching him as he spoke, seeing the pain he was feeling and knowing it was kin to what was in her own heart.

He walked over to the tall window, laced his hands behind his back, and began to speak. He answered all her questions before he finished—all but one. "She died of pneumonia, brought on by exposure. She's buried very near the spot where we found her, by the double oaks over to the east. I'll take you there. It happened seven months ago."

"Why did you bury her there?"

"Because they don't allow—" There was a long pause, which Landra dared not break into. The dangerous stiffness to his back, the overcharged quality in the very air made her stay silent. Suddenly he turned to face her. "They don't allow suicides to be buried there."

As though he had struck her, she stepped back from him. "Not Bethany . . . I don't believe it!"

There was a strangled sound of protest from the doorway, and Landra realized they were not alone, that Lucas Delacroix had not left. Adam said, "Lucas, go downstairs and wait for me." Even in her own turmoil Landra could see the effect the words, spoken with such cold authority, had on the younger man. He flushed, and shot a look that was very near hatred at Adam. He covered it well, and she thought perhaps Adam hadn't seen it, or if he had, was unaffected by it. Lucas turned and left.

"Adam, if Bethany died of pneumonia, how can you say it was suicide?"

"She . . . she hadn't been well for quite some time, and was terribly depressed. One day last fall she went out into the rain and lay down between the double oaks. I didn't find her for several hours, and by the time I did, she had developed pneumonia." He squeezed his eyes shut and a choking noise forced itself from his lips. "She only lasted until the next evening. She died in this room, in this bed." He walked over to the elaborate bed and stroked the dark blue velvet coverlet absently for a few seconds, then said, "That priest, Father Etienne, heard her confession."

"Why, Adam, why would my sister . . . your wife, do such a thing? She had everything she'd ever wanted, everything to live for—"

"I can't tell you."

"But—"

"You'll have to trust me!"

"That's what you said before, trust you, and be patient. But you lied to me, and you're still withholding something." She took a deep breath. "And I saw you today with that awful woman, Carrie Chaumont. Oh, Adam, how can I trust you?"

"Then don't," he said wearily. "But stay out of my way. I've got things to do, important things, and time is running out. As for Carrie Chaumont, you don't know her. I'll be frank with you, Landra—"

"I wish you would," she interrupted.

He finished his statement through clenched teeth. "I've got people coming at me from all sides, and you are just one more distraction. Stay, if you insist, but keep out of my laboratory, and let Rose alone. My work is all I have left now."

"And what about Carrie Chaumont?"

"She has nothing to do with any of this." He looked at her keenly. "What would you do if I told you everything, as you insist?"

"I wouldn't have any qualms about going to the proper authorities if I thought it was necessary." That same recklessness shone from her eyes, more than plain for him to see. "Adam, who are those people downstairs? What are they doing here?"

"They're my patients."

"What are you treating them for?"

"Please, Landra, I can't answer your questions, don't you see, *I can't!*" He strode angrily from the room, leaving Landra limp and exhausted, and absolutely certain that the remark about Carrie Chaumont had been just one more lie. She went slowly to her room, feeling hurt and bruised.

Lying on the bed that she had shared with Bethany so long ago, Landra stared up at the ceiling, at the cobwebs which hung there, and the unsightly mold in one corner. The roof must leak over that spot, she thought, and my sister is dead. She deliberately lay in the rain until she got pneumonia. That's why Father Etienne had been so evasive. Bethany had confessed to him, had asked for God's forgiveness, and had died.

Landra knew the priest would die, too, before he divulged the reason for Bethany's suicide. The word echoed in her mind. She could not imagine what terrible circumstance would drive Bethany to want to end her life. Wasn't what Landra had said earlier true? Hadn't Bethany had everything a woman could want?

The sudden image of the two dark heads, drawn close together there on the terrace at Elkhorn this morning, flashed into her mind and would not leave.

CHAPTER 7

It was late evening when Landra descended the circular staircase. True to her word, Rose had brought a tray up, and Landra had eaten the food and placed the tray outside the door, but she couldn't have said what had been on it. Now she was intent only on finding Adam.

But it was Lucas who stood in the shadowed hallway. "He's gone." His words were curiously flat, devoid of feeling.

Landra said, "You don't like Dr. Jarrett." When he did not speak she went on, "I think it has something to do with my sister."

He stared hard at her; then his expression changed. "I loved her," he said softly.

Landra was not surprised; every man she met was charmed by Bethany. "Did she know?"

"If you mean did I ever tell her, no. She was too fine, too good; and she loved him." He stopped, then said almost reverently, "But I think she knew how I felt about her."

Landra nodded. "A woman does. Where did Adam go? Do you know?"

As though he hadn't heard her, Lucas said, "Once I thought he was almost a god. But since she died he's driven himself, and us, until—" The bitterness was back.

"His research, you mean, his work? What is it all about, Dr. Delacroix?

He shook his head. "I can't tell you that. We have to be very careful, especially now. They—"

"The other doctors, from New Orleans, perhaps? Rose said something about them."

"Rose is afraid for Jimmy. He's all she cares about."

"And you? What do you care about?"

"The project. It's mine, too, you know."

Landra tried to pin down the quality in his tone, but failed. "Dr. Delacroix," she began, "what is this 'project'? What—"

He cut her off abruptly. "I've got to go."

"Then at least you can tell me where he's gone—if you know."

He looked at her steadily. "The same place he's gone every day for almost a year, now. To *her* house." He left before Landra could ask who, but she really didn't need to. She knew.

Retrieving a shawl from her room, she went outside, with no real plan except to find Adam. The day birds were twitting sleepily, and here and there she could hear a mockingbird tuning up. It was, after all these years, home. Still undecided as to what to do, she stepped from the shadowed veranda and was surprised to hear the whinny of a horse. She could just make out the outline of a carriage at the end of the drive. Then it began to move toward her, and when she saw it was Hollis she cried out gladly.

"Hollis! I'm so glad you've come!"

"Come? I've been here most of the afternoon, keeping an eye on things."

"That's wonderful of you." She looked at the grin on his face, and couldn't help but smile back.

"I'm glad you think so. Now, where do you want to go?"

"To Carrie Chaumont's," she answered, her voice small, the smile gone. "But I don't know where she lives, and how did you know I wanted to go somewhere?"

He shrugged. "Maybe I just wanted to take you someplace," he said, his eyes warm. "And it so happens I went to see Denis, and he told me where she lives. Took some doing, I must say. He's awfully closemouthed, isn't he?"

At his steady gaze Landra felt a little flustered; she took off her gloves and tucked them into the reticule which hung at her wrist. "Yes, he certainly is. He let me know the other day that he felt gossip is for women, and he wanted no part of it. I'm never quite sure what goes over the line and should be considered gossip, and what is just—"

"Useful information?" he supplied as he helped her into the carriage.

She heard the teasing note in his voice but felt too disturbed to respond as she told him what she'd found out from Lucas Delacroix, and Adam.

He listened without breaking in and when she had finished, he said gravely, "And you believe, more than ever, that he's involved with this Carrie Chaumont, that his involvement caused her suicide?"

"Yes, and I can hardly bear the thought. It seems impossible!"

He clucked to the horse and the carriage moved away from Greenlea. "I take it the last time you saw them your sister and Dr. Jarrett were very much in love."

"More than anyone I've ever known," said Landra softly. "I used to daydream about finding someone who would love me as Adam loves—loved—" She broke off, tears choking her throat.

Hollis took the reins in one hand and put his free arm around her shoulder. "There, it's going to get easier, but it'll take time."

She leaned against his warm strength. "You're very kind." Suddenly she straightened and pulled away. "Please forgive me. You mustn't think I'm . . . that I act this familiarly with every man I meet. Believe me, I don't." Landra withdrew a tiny square of lace from the reticule and dabbed her eyes.

"I never thought otherwise," Hollis said earnestly. "This is a very difficult time for you, and you need a friend. I want to be that friend, Landra, if you'll let me."

Landra searched his face in the gathering dusk, then said, her voice very low, "I appreciate that more than I can tell you. The past few years have been difficult, Hollis. If I don't seem to be following the rules of etiquette, it isn't just because of the situation, unusual as it is. There wasn't much time for social . . . for—"

"You aren't going to try to tell me there weren't hordes of suitors buzzing about, vying for your hand? Because if you are, I won't believe it."

With a sigh Landra said, "Believe it. Nursing my mother was a full-time job, and she wasn't a demanding, irascible patient, either. She was like Beth—kind, soft-spoken, and gentle . . . all the things I'm not. Now, if she'd been like me, she'd probably have been impossibly difficult."

"I'd be delighted to have you as a patient, impossible or not." He hastened to add, "But don't get sick; I'd rather have you as my friend." He patted her shoulder lightly. "Carrie Chaumont's house is there, on the left. Do you want me to go inside with you?"

They were on the other side of town now, and Landra thought

briefly, resentfully, that in its isolation the little cottage was perfect for a meeting place.

"No, I don't think so. But thank you, and thank you for all you've done."

"Only the beginning, I assure you. And I'll be right here if you need me." He twisted the reins around the post at Carrie Chaumont's gate, and settled back to wait.

Reminded of Denis, she smiled, then turned toward the house. The smile faded. It was no easy thing to walk up to the door and knock.

Carrie Chaumont was even more beautiful up close. The soft glow of lamplight outlined her small, graceful body; she wore a dress of sea-green with a low, scooped neckline framed in white lace. Landra felt huge and hot in the high-necked black silk. She started to speak, but words failed her as she looked past the woman and into the room. There, seated in a low, armless rocker, was Adam. In his arms he held a child, a beautiful child with a riot of dark curls, laughing in delight as Adam made a ridiculous face.

"Adam!" she cried out. Startled, he turned to face her. Landra swept past Carrie Chaumont, and as she came to stand by the chair, the child looked up at her. His eyes were deep blue, his mouth sweetly red. Suddenly he laughed again and held up dimpled, fat little hands to Landra, who instinctively reached down and took his soft body in her arms. The baby was about a year old, and smelled of powder and sun-dried clothes; as he picked industriously at the brooch fastened to her dress, Landra looked into his round, dimpled face.

But it was, after all, just a baby's face. She tightened her arms and the child let out an indignant squeal. Quickly Carrie stepped over and took him. "Now, now, Robert—little Rob. You're fine," she crooned, her voice low and sweet. He gurgled at her, and tucked his head under her chin, still watching Landra coyly.

Landra fought to keep her voice steady as she spoke. "Is he your son, Adam?" He stood, and Landra stepped back to look at him, unwilling to tilt her head as she'd watched Carrie do that morning. "Is he?" she asked again.

"Yes, he is." He met her eyes squarely, with no shame, no remorse.

"And all the times you've come here in the past year, it was to see—" She looked at the woman who stood quietly with the baby in her arms. "And Bethany knew." She could feel the tears stinging behind her eyelids; she could not bear crying in front of them. "I never heard of anything so despicable!" She rushed out the door to the waiting Hollis Freman.

"Come on, now," he said as he led her to the carriage. "It can't be that bad."

"It's worse! No wonder my sister killed herself. He's monstrous. I hate him—*I hate him!*"

He helped her into the carriage, then drove aimlessly around until she could put into words what she'd just found out at Carrie Chaumont's. He refrained from commenting; her anger was deep and cold, and instinctively he knew she did not want his advice. Finally he said, "Do you want to go to the Chaumonts' for the night?"

Landra shook her head firmly. "No, Hollis, I want to go back to Greenlea and wait for him. Tomorrow I intend to see a lawyer, and it's only fair that I warn him."

"See a lawyer? What about?"

"To see what can be done about getting him out of Greenlea! After what he's done, you can't imagine I'd want him to stay— that he has any right to be there—"

"But even so, he was her husband. He surely has some legal rights," Hollis protested as they drew near Greenlea.

"Not if I can help it. My mother was the sole inheritor of Greenlea, and she never legally deeded it to Bethany, only told her it was hers . . . and Adam's." There was a telltale catch in her throat, but Landra went on stubbornly. "I don't know about wills and things, but it would seem to me that it's at least half mine—maybe all. Anyway, tomorrow I intend to find out."

"And what about tonight?" The worry was obvious in his voice. "I don't think you should stay there, especially if what you say is true."

"*If* it's true!"

"Why, yes; now that I'm sort of involved, I've been remembering some of the things my grandfather told me."

"What things?"

"That your Dr. Jarrett's a hardworking, dedicated man," Hollis said. They had come around the oyster-shell drive, and he stopped the horse before the front entrance and came around to help her down.

"That could very well be true. In fact, I'm certain it is," Landra admitted. "But being hardworking and dedicated doesn't prevent a man from being unfaithful, from driving his wife to suicide!"

"You don't know that's so—"

"How can you defend him?" Landra blazed. "You should have seen him with that baby, the baby that should have been my sister's!"

"Did you give him a chance to explain?"

"Explain what? How he found someone else to . . . to—" A wail escaped Landra's lips and she crumpled, her anger giving way to anguish.

Stricken, Hollis watched as her shoulders shook with silent sobs; then he reached out his hands toward her. "Don't, Landra," he whispered, "please don't." He held her hands until the tears subsided, thinking, a little dazedly, how fresh and lovely she was as she stepped out of the carriage.

She lifted her head slowly, her mouth trembling with a new emotion now. "Hollis, I . . ." He kissed her cheek so lightly, so tenderly that when she closed her eyes it was like the touch of a butterfly. Landra felt lightheaded, giddy, wonderfully weak.

Hollis tucked her arm through his and turned toward the house. His voice was rough with feeling as he said, "Oh, Landra, I don't know just how, but it will all come right. We don't know all the facts yet, and besides, don't ever forget that God is in control, and that He cares."

The lovely mood shattered for her; Landra stiffened and pulled away. "How can you be so sure? If He cares, if He's interested in what goes on, then why did He let such terrible things happen to my sister?"

"You're not being reasonable or fair, Landra."

"It's God who's not fair! Bethany, of all people, was the least one to ever deserve to be . . . betrayed!" She jerked away from Hollis. "And when you say God is right for allowing all this to happen and . . . and you defend Adam, you aren't any better than he is!"

With that she whirled and ran to the big, old cypress door, forgetting it had been locked before. It wasn't now, however, and she was grateful that her rather theatrical exit wasn't thwarted; the door swung open and she slipped inside. She stood with her back to it, fighting a battle with tears again, thinking with anger, and yes, of regret, of the awful scene with Hollis. How unfair it was that women are encouraged to give vent to their feelings, and men trained to a stoical repression of tears!

At every crisis, large or small, the tears stung and threatened . . . even when she'd first gazed into that baby's angelic face.

The baby. Little Rob, the woman had called him. Adam's baby. Slowly she climbed the stairs, went into the dark bedroom where Bethany had died, and then into the nursery. There was a candle on the small white chest. With shaking fingers she lit it and looked around. A maple crib stood by the window, complete with sheets and lovely hand-made quilts, topped by a gossamer—a light, knitted shawl of pale blue.

She opened the drawers. In neat piles were shirts and kimonos, dozens of diapers, and more intricately embroidered blankets and quilts than six babies could use. Landra closed the drawers quietly and sat in the high-backed rocker next to the crib.

Bethany had always wanted a child. Had she sat in this chair and stitched one tiny garment and quilt after another, hoping Adam would come to her and give her a beautiful, black-haired son—like Rob? Perhaps she had realized she would never be able to bear him a son, had even known somehow about Carrie Chaumont . . . Perhaps that was why she had decided she couldn't face life any longer. The tears rolled down Landra's cheeks; silently she vowed to make him pay for what he had done to Bethany. In her mind a quiet voice spoke, one from a long-ago Sunday school lesson: *Vengeance is mine.* It cut through her like a knife.

"But, God," she whispered fiercely, "it isn't fair! Bethany didn't deserve this; she deserved only good! Why, God . . . *why?*" Landra wanted badly to understand; she tried to pray, to ask for understanding. But no matter how hard she tried, no answers came. The faith of her father was just that. His faith, not hers. She had survived her mother's long illness, even the death of both her parents, with that second-hand faith, but it would not serve her now. She could think of nothing but the total injustice of the situation, could not rationalize away the inequity of it. Bitterness crept in, making her grind her teeth with the futility both of things as they were and of things unknown as well. There were no tears now, only a dry-eyed, hard resolution to avenge her sister. How long she sat in the darkening room she never knew. Finally, the soft, insistent voice of Rose startled her from the trance-like state into which she had fallen.

"Ma'am," she said, "please—"

Landra looked up, her eyes straining in the dimness. The

candle had burned completely away. "Who is it?" she asked uncertainly.

"Rose, and I need help." Each hand was twisting the fingers of the other in turn.

"What's wrong?"

"It's Jimmy, his eyes," she answered, a painful agitation edging her words. "He's bad, worse than I've ever seen him. Dr. Adam isn't here, and there's no more medicine for the pain, and I have to go and find him!" she finished in a breathless rush.

Fully alert now, Landra rose and drew a deep breath. "What is it that you want me to do?"

"It helps if he has hot packs on his eyes. Please, will you help?"

"Of course I will, Rose," she said as she followed the girl, who was already moving away. They had almost reached the door to the kitchen when Landra halted.

"Come on," urged Rose. "Please!"

"Rose, that other man, the one I saw the first night I came, did he have an accident of some sort, or . . . or was he in the war?"

"Yes," she said eagerly, "he was in the war; he fought in Cuba. That's it, the war. You're not afraid of him, are you?"

Landra hesitated, then said slowly, "Yes, I guess I am. It's not that I don't want to help, but why can't *he* prepare the hot packs for Jimmy?"

Rose took her arm and almost pulled her down the hallway that led to the converted study-laboratory. "It's his hands, Miss Cole, his hands are . . . oh, please hurry!"

The room they entered bore no resemblance whatever to the cozy book-lined study Landra remembered. The wall of an adjoining room had been knocked out to form one long, white-walled space. The odor in the place rushed at Landra, surrounded her, clung to her. Merely noticeable in the huge bedroom and nursery upstairs, here it was palpable, an evil, living thing.

She gasped. "Rose, what is that dreadful odor?"

"It's something Dr. Adam is working on, a treatment." Rose indicated with a wave of her hand the high, long table which held numerous flasks, beakers and tubes. The low, agonized sound of a man moaning caught the attention of both women.

"Jimmy darlin', Jimmy, I'm here!" Rose rushed to kneel by the cot on which the young man lay, his hands pressed tightly to a cloth covering his eyes. There was but one small lamp lit, placed on a desk which had been Landrum Cole's. The desk was at the opposite end of the room from where Jimmy lay, the walls on three sides around it covered with books from floor to ceiling.

Landra watched as Rose changed the cloth, soaking it in a basin into which she had poured hot water from a kettle, then wringing it almost dry and placing it tenderly on Jimmy's eyes. The boy—for Landra thought he must scarcely be twenty years old—could not, though he tried, suppress the groans of pain.

Rose came away from him reluctantly. "You see, Miss Cole, it's not hard. It's the only thing that helps except the morphia, and Dr. Adam will give that to him only when it's really bad." Another stifled moan brought the girl to Jimmy's side once more. "There, darlin', I'll be back with Dr. Adam as soon as I can." She held his shivering body close for one long moment, then was gone before Landra could protest.

She sat in the straight-backed chair by his bedside, only getting up to put on more water to heat or to change the cloth on his eyes. Once they fluttered open and he saw the faint outline of her face; saw that she was not Rose. After that he tried even harder to muffle the cries that strained his throat. He was a handsome boy, his dark brown hair wavy and trimmed close. Landra realized with a pang that Rose had probably performed even this small service; had carefully, if inexpertly, cut the hair of the young man she loved so desperately and could not marry.

Why not? Landra had only a moment to wonder when Jimmy's hand clutched suddenly at the bedcovering, his knuckles white. Impulsively she took it in her own, the stab of pity she felt so strong it took her breath. He was suffering so terribly. Almost without thinking she began to sing in a low, tremulous voice. The song was not one she chose consciously; it was one from the most distant memories of childhood, one her father had lulled her to sleep with countless times. It may have been the only song she knew by heart.

"Jesus loves me, this I know,
For the Bible tells me so
Little ones to Him belong,
They are weak, but He is strong.
Yes, Jesus loves me,
Yes, Jesus loves me;
Yes, Jesus loves me,
The Bible tells me so."

Her voice, never strong, wavered as she finished the chorus and the pressure she felt from Jimmy's hand tightened.

He whispered, "He doesn't love me."

"Jimmy, of course He does!"

"No."

The word was so forlorn, so final; Landra placed her hand on the boy's burning cheek. "Jesus does love you, Jimmy. He does care."

Jimmy struggled upright, the warm cloth falling from his eyes. The look of anguished pain in his dark eyes tore at her, and when Jimmy spoke she had difficulty breathing. "Then why did he do this to me? *Why?*"

"I . . ." Landra hesitated, unable to take her eyes from Jimmy's searching ones. Her own doubting, angry thoughts of less than an hour ago came back to haunt her. Finally she said slowly, "Jimmy, surely you know God didn't do this to you. He doesn't make bad things happen to people. He loves us. God is good, He . . . He *is* love." She was all too aware that even now she was parroting words, repeating what she had been told. Did she really believe what she said? Unwilling to face that question, she gently replaced the cloth on his eyes as he sank back.

It was a long while before Jimmy spoke again. "Then why did He let me get sick? If He didn't make me sick, He *let* me!"

Stricken, Landra had no answer. Why, indeed? Why had God allowed her sister to fall into such hard circumstances, and why was this boy in such terrible pain? *Why?*

The cloth had cooled, and she rose to heat another. In the few moments that passed, the desperate statement Jimmy had uttered hung in the warm, still air. Then, as she took her place beside the suffering boy, she placed the cloth on his eyes again with infinite gentleness, and took his hand in hers again. "I'm here, Jimmy. You're not alone, I'm here." His fingers grasped hers tightly.

"I . . . I'm so afraid. . . . My eyes, I don't want to lose my sight!"

"Hush, try to calm yourself," Landra soothed, wanting desperately to help him, knowing she could not. She felt so totally helpless, and somehow she knew Jimmy felt her helplessness. His well-shaped mouth distorted with a recurring onslaught of pain, and his face flushed a dark red. Landra could only guess, but from the experience of nursing her mother, she estimated his temperature at several degrees above a hundred.

What could be causing it? Obviously his eyes were affected; his symptoms were puzzling to say the least. Rose had said the other man had been in Cuba, but Jimmy was too young. And Rose herself—there was nothing wrong with her that Landra could see. Perhaps she was only here because of Jimmy. It was all so strange. If only Adam had explained. She wished she could talk to Jimmy further, to question him about his illness. But the pain, like a clawing beast, tore at the helpless boy, leaving him limp and exhausted.

Minutes dribbled into hours, and Landra had no idea how many times she replaced the hot packs on Jimmy's eyes. It was very quiet in the room, and up to now she had really not considered the fact that she was alone in the house with no one but Jimmy—and the faceless man.

She did not hear him enter the room, but she knew he was standing behind her before she heard him speak.

"Rose is . . . gone?" The words were harsh, guttural, even more frightening to Landra than they had been in the old kitchen. For Rose was gone, and he knew it.

CHAPTER 8

She whirled around. In the flickering lamplight she could see the man with terrible clarity. He had no eyebrows or eyelashes; his forehead had great shining reddish welts, some of which were open sores. His nose was wrecked, the nostrils distended and swollen. Through lips that were swollen as badly as his nostrils came the same words again. "Rose is gone." There was a queer, terrifying, hoarse quality about it, almost sepulchral. It was like being spoken to by a dead man.

"Please . . . what do you want?" Landra inched backward, and even as she did so, he came imperceptibly closer. She was soon flat against the cold, white wall. The terrible odor was very strong now; he seemed to exude it. He extended his hands to her, and Landra could see the ugly, claw-like things coming toward her. "No! Leave me alone!" She put her own hands up to shield her face.

He took a step backward, and Landra heard him utter two deep, almost unrecognizable words from deep within his throat. He said them over and over, until she thought, *Is it possible he's saying "I'm sorry"?* And then, she was sure. Somehow she knew he was apologizing for . . . just being what he was, for frightening her. Incredulously she watched as he went and sat beside the boy on the bed, and though his face was a ghastly ruin, she knew the expression there was pity. This wreck of a man felt pity for Jimmy!

Weakly she let her hands fall to her sides. It was time to change the wet pack, and she steeled herself as she reached for it. Her eyes met those of the man, and he nodded slowly.

She understood suddenly that he would do it gladly for Jimmy if he were able, but he was not; she saw now what Rose had

83

meant. His hands were twisted grotesquely and she doubted that he could even hold the cloths, much less wring them out. He was glad and grateful that she was willing to do it. It was all in his eyes, those dark eyes which held her own and spoke so eloquently; of total empathy with Jimmy, of her own helplessness and fear, and something more. His eyes spoke of a suffering she had never known, and would never experience. Suffering had made the man before her—wrecked though he was by something more terrible than her imagination could fathom—someone she could no longer fear. She could see the strength in him, the compassion for Jimmy even when he himself was far worse than his young friend. A smile trembled at her lips as she stood aside when he rose from the bed, walked slowly to the other side of the room, and sat down to keep watch.

There were dark curtains at the windows, but one was open slightly. Landra must have slept, for she came upright in her chair when she heard Jimmy scream. "The light . . . please shut out the light! I can't bear it!" She jumped to her feet and yanked the curtain shut. Hurrying to replenish the hot water, she saw that the man who had been slumped against the far wall was gone. Had she merely dreamed he was there? Had she conjured him up in the dead of night, made him fearsome, then harmless?

A muffled moan from Jimmy brought her to him, the hot, moist pack ready. She was sitting once more with her hand in his when Adam burst into the room, Rose close behind. He had not shaved and his black hair was untidy. Totally oblivious to Landra, he came over to where Jimmy lay.

"Jimmy, boy. Has it been bad?" He felt the pack, nodded approvingly and said to Rose, "Get my bag, please."

Landra rose stiffly and went to the door. He'd not come home all night, she realized; she'd left him at *her* place, and it was now dawn. Suddenly she couldn't bear to even be in the same house with him.

"Adam, I'll need a carriage," she said coldly. He didn't answer, for Rose had handed him his black bag and he was rummaging about in it, intent on finding something. She cleared her throat and said again, more loudly, "I'll need a carriage. There's some business I have to take care of in town—"

"What? Oh, a carriage." He frowned. "Take it. I left it outside; the horse is still hitched up." He went on filling a hypodermic syringe without looking at her again.

In a daze she walked through the house and up to her room, stopping only long enough to wash her face and get her reticule.

The slow, plodding horse could have been the same one that brought her to Greenlea . . . how long ago? Could it be possible it was only three days? She blinked wearily at the rising sun. The nearer she drew to town, the more she realized it was far too early to be making a business call, that she had acted rashly in leaving the house so quickly. And she hadn't told Adam what she planned to do.

But then, he'd not really cared what she was doing; he'd not even thanked her for taking care of his precious patient. She sniffed noisily, wallowing for a brief moment in self-pity, until she thought of Jimmy. She hadn't cared for him because of Adam, but because the boy's need had fairly screamed at her. Perhaps she was, after all, a nurse. Her mother's physician, Dr. Atwood, had said repeatedly she had the heart and hands of a good nurse.

When she came even with the Chaumont house, she reined over and got down. At her light knock Mrs. Chaumont came at once, and Landra knew she had probably been up for at least an hour. She had laughingly told Landra that the only time she could be by herself was before the herd, as she affectionately called Denis and her three little daughters, got up and started thundering.

"Why, it's Landra," she said, pleased and surprised at the same time. "Come in, child! You look as frashed as you were that night Denis brought you, and here it is early morning."

"I know, and I'm sorry. If I could just stay for a little while until things in town open up . . . I have an important errand." She caught hold of the door facing, feeling slightly faint.

As with most redheads, her skin was pale, almost translucent. It was very white, now, and the shadows under her green eyes alarmed Mrs. Chaumont. She put her arm around the drooping girl and led her to the couch in the small living room. She lifted her feet and asked if her stays were too tight. When Landra murmured no, the older woman hurried off to the kitchen, to return shortly with a steaming cup of the tisane.

"Here, drink this. I'll get you a pillow and a quilt. You need sleep."

"But I've got business to attend to . . ." She trailed off, and obediently took a sip of the potent brew.

"There's nothing that can't wait until you've had some rest."
Mrs. Chaumont spread a faded, fragrant sun-dried quilt over
Landra, and in a short time she fell asleep.

When she awakened, Landra could tell by the brightness of
the sunshine it was late morning. She started to sit up, anxious
to be out and doing something. But she heard voices—Denis
and Mrs. Chaumont. They were on the porch swing, next to the
open window where Landra lay on the couch.

"Is she still asleep?" asked Denis.

"Yes, I'm sure she is. I'm worried about her. You know how
she looked that first day—"

"Do I! An angel, a beautiful vision!"

"Denis!" The voice of a girl broke in, and Landra wondered
if it were Katy.

Denis' next words confirmed it. "Now Katy-love, you're my
girl, and no red-haired angel could change that." Katy made a
funny little self-satisfied sound in response.

"As I was saying," Mrs. Chaumont went on, "after only a
day and night at that place, she looks downright poorly."

"You . . . you don't supppose she's caught it already?"

"Aw, Katy," Denis protested, "don't say that! It's only ru-
mors; anyway, we don't know if what they say about Dr. Jarrett
is true."

"They say Dr. Jarrett's been helping the other one, Dr. Dyer,
that's running things. One's as bad as the other. I don't trust
him. And no one is really sure what happened to his wife—"

"Katy!" broke in Denis. "She might hear you. Hush up!"

But Landra was already standing at the door, her hair tumbled about her shoulders, the black of her dress contrasting
sharply with the pale oval of her face. "What are you talking
about?"

Mrs. Chaumont's eyes were troubled, her smooth brow
marred by a deep frown. She held her bottom lip tightly between her teeth, and did not reply to Landra's question. Beside
her on the swing sat a young girl with long, pale yellow hair
hanging on her shoulders. She had a pretty face, a china-doll
face, and Landra could see why Denis adored her. But the wide,
violet-blue eyes were fixed on Landra, and the expression in
them was fear. She jumped up, crossed herself hastily, and with
one last terrified glance at Landra, ran down the steps and out
of the yard.

"Katy! Come back here!" But she did not even look back as

Denis called to her. For a moment he stood undecided, then with an apologetic glance at Landra, ran after the girl.

Landra followed Mrs. Chaumont into the kitchen and watched as she carefully folded and refolded a tea towel three times. She could tell the woman was avoiding her eyes. "Mrs. Chaumont—"

"Call me Rene. My name is Rene, but Will—he was my man—he always called me Renie." Finally, she met Landra's eyes.

"Please tell me what you and Denis and Katy were talking about. I couldn't help but overhear. What is Katy afraid I've caught, and who is Dr. Dyer?"

Slowly Rene said, "He's a doctor at the medical school, over in New Orelans."

"What kind of doctor?" Landra persisted.

"Oh, a der . . . derma . . ."

"Dermatologist?"

"That's it, I heard it at the market."

"What else did you hear?" Landra looked straight into the woman's eyes, willing her to answer.

"That they've bought Elkhorn plantation, right next to your home, and they're going to make it into a hospital." Reluctance was plain on her face.

Landra felt a vague, cold fear. "Go on, Rene; *who* bought it, and what kind of hospital?"

"A . . . they say for . . . Oh, Landra, I can't be *sure* it's true! I'd hate myself if I was the one to tell you and it wasn't true. You can see how it is, can't you? If it isn't, and *I* was the one who told you, I'd never forgive myself! I don't want to spread malicious gossip; it's something I hate, and I've tried to teach my children the same thing. Can you understand?"

She looked enormously relieved when Jeannette burst into the room. "Mama, Mama, can Joyuese and Jolie and me go and pick dewberries over to Tish's? Please, can we, huh?" She danced about, flashing a winsome smile at Landra. "I'll bake you a pie, Miss Landra," she said as her mother climbed on a chair to reach the berry baskets.

By the time the child left, Landra had come to a decision. It was time she went back to New Orleans and found someone who knew what was going on. Surely Hollis would take her to the university. Rene Chaumont was obviously extremely discomfited by her questions, and felt, as Denis had, that it was not her place to inform Landra. Calmly she said to her, "I'm leaving now. Thank you again for taking care of me."

"You'll come back, now, won't you?" asked Rene anxiously, feeling she had let Landra down by not answering her questions, but bound by a code stronger than her pity for the young woman.

"Yes, I'll be back," said Landra with a wan smile, "if only to get some more of that wonderful gumbo." She understood, and even admired Rene's strength of character, but felt a painful urgency to get at the truth—whatever it was.

Outside, the day was bright and hot, the temperature hovering at ninety and the humidity not far behind. Landra saw that someone, probably Denis, had unhitched the horse and tethered him nearby in the shade of a large chinaberry tree. She smiled briefly as she thought of the endless wars she and Bethany had engaged in with the hard, round, green chinaberries as ammunition. Bethany had always given up first. . . .

It took less time than she thought to hitch the horse to the small buggy. She wasn't quite sure it was done properly, but perhaps it would hold. Her face, by this time, was covered with a fine film of perspiration. The sun beat down, its powerful rays absorbed and held by the black fabric of her dress. She stepped up into the buggy, grateful for the small shade its top afforded.

As she drove slowly into town, she wondered at the unusual number of people. They were clumped here and there in little groups, talking excitedly. There was an electric quality to the atmosphere, as if little shocks of emotion had sprung from one mind and mouth to another, like sparks jump the space between live wires.

A great many of them had newspapers, and jabbed frequently at them with indignant fingers. She stopped the horse near three men who stood in front of the small red brick bank building. One of them, a tall, thin man dressed in a somber suit with a face to match, shook his head and said, "They came in my bank, here," he nodded his head at the staid building behind him, "and wanted to borrow money to finance their hellish scheme. I told them no, of course," he hastened to add, as the broad, ugly man beside him glared angrily.

"I reckon you better, Jason," he said, " 'less you want a whole colony of *them* at Elkhorn—practically at your doorstep. They may call it a hospital, those doctors, but any fool knows it's nothin' but a—" He stopped as he caught sight of Landra.

She couldn't keep herself from leaning over and calling out to the men. "I beg your pardon, but could you please give me some information?"

Even pale and fatigued as she was, she was still beautiful enough to cause the men to stop and stare until one of them, the banker they called Jason, stepped over and said, "What can I do for you, Miss—"

"Miss Cole, Landra Cole."

He looked at her sharply. "You wouldn't be Bethany Jarrett's little sister by any chance?"

"Yes," she said, aware of the change in his expression as she spoke.

He nodded slowly. "We'd heard you were in town. You've been staying out to Greenlea? With *them*?" He took a step backward. The other men were watching closely, their eyes narrowed at her.

"Why, yes, but only since yesterday. What is this all about?"

The banker snatched a newspaper from one of the other men and thrust it at Landra; then, all three of them moved away, talking to the people in front of the building next door, pointing as the did so back at Landra.

Frightened now, she unfolded the newspaper he had given her. It was a New Orleans paper, the *Daily Picayune*. Nothing had prepared her for what she saw there in a bold, black, ugly headline:

DYER DOOMS ELKHORN PLANTATION TO LEPERS!!!!

CHAPTER 9

The date was May 18, 1901, and the story below the headline was long and detailed. A protective numbness stole over Landra as she read it.

> Dr. Isodore Dyer, lecturer on dermatology at Tulane University, has for some time worked tirelessly to persuade the Louisiana legislature to appropriate money for a leper home, and was responsible for the creation of a Board of Control to realize this project.
>
> Seven years ago, an asylum was set up at Indian Camp Plantation following the secret negotiations that led to the state's taking a five-year lease on the property.

Landra skimmed over the description of the home at Indian Camp; how the first patients were taken down the river on a barge under cover of night, how they were the refugees from a "pest hole" in New Orleans on Hagan Street. Three of them had refused to go.

> Dr. Dyer feels the location of the leper home at Indian Camp is ill advised, located as it is so far away from our cities. Without the benefit of Tulane's School of Tropical Medicine nearby, and the University's laboratory facilities, the study and perhaps the cure for Hansen's disease (or as it is more commonly known, leprosy) will be seriously hampered, says Dr. Dyer. Dr. Dyer recently resigned as president of the Board of Control because of the opposition of a majority of his colleagues.
>
> Dr. Dyer and Mr. Albert G. Phelps, who succeeded him as president of the Board, have brought pressure on the state legislature, which has appropriated $25,000 to acquire and equip a suitable site for a permanent leprosarium.
>
> This "suitable site" is our own Elkhorn plantation, in Jefferson Parish, just across the Mississippi from our great and

fair city of New Orleans. The final negotiations were completed late last night. . . .

Late last night. The article did not mention Adam, but Landra knew now where he had been—with the grave young doctor whose face stared from the newspaper: Dr. Isodore Dyer. It was the face of the man she'd seen with Adam and Carrie at Elkhorn.

Slowly, she picked up her purse and drew the strings, placed it on her wrist and stepped from the buggy. She walked along the sidewalk, trying to ignore the whispers.

"Jason says that's Mrs. Jarrett's sister."

"Purty, ain't she?"

"Yeah, but it don't show, right at first. Think she's got it, too?"

"They say he's keeping three of them lepers right out there at Greenlea."

"Nobody's seen Miz Jarrett for a mighty long time, now. Do you suppose—"

One woman's voice was harsher, more strident than the others, with all the assurance of the permanently self-righteous. "Leprosy is a judgment of God! It's a punishment for sin!" At that Landra turned. The woman was as tall as she, her gaunt face pulled and made uglier by the tight gray bun pinned high on her head. Her eyes were small, black, and stared intently into Landra's shocked face.

"You don't know what you're saying—" Landra choked.

"Think not?" she retorted; then both turned as a commotion began down the street. "It's them!" she cried. "It's them—let's show 'em what we think about a leper home in our backyard!"

Two men emerged from one of the buildings. Landra recognized one as the man she'd seen at Elkhorn, the man whose face was in the newspaper clutched in her hand—Dr. Dyer. Close by his side was Adam Jarrett, looking even grimmer than when she'd confronted him with the knowledge that Bethany was dead. But he did not look afraid, not even when the woman who'd been shouting stopped to pick up a clod of dirt from the street and threw it, screaming in satisfaction when it spattered against the whiteness of his shirt.

Others began scrabbling for rocks, dirt, anything to throw; the scene became something from a nightmare. The heat stifled Landra, and she could scarcely breathe. Dimly she was aware of the fear and rage emanating from the mob; she heard their shouts and screams only distantly. She was jostled and carried along; but she scarcely felt it somehow. She was separate, apart from them, apart from her own body. The only reality was in her mind.

The three wretched souls with whom she'd passed the endless night were lepers. *Lepers!* The very word sent a wrenching shudder through her body. Rose, and Jimmy—poor, blind, helpless Jimmy, whose hot face and eyes she'd bathed, whose clutching hand she'd held—and the rotting, ruined man who had no face!

Bethany, the gay, beautiful, golden-haired girl who'd only wanted to love Adam and give him babies ... he'd brought those creatures into her home, brought the dread disease close enough to infect his own wife. No wonder he'd turned from her to Carrie Chaumont, if she had come to look like that man whose clawed, ugly hands had reached out to Landra last night. Her horror was so deep she felt as though she was under water, beyond sight and sound of the angry mob around her.

The sound of a gunshot shocked her out of the trance-like state, and Adam suddenly crumpled to the ground. Someone had shot Adam! Though she would have thought it impossible, the confusion and noise became even greater then, and her panic grew as the crowd pushed and shoved in an attempt to see the fallen man.

"Please, let me through—" For answer a woman roughly shoved her so that she almost fell to the ground; she would have except for the press of hot, crazed bodies around her. "Adam . . ."

The sound of her voice was lost, and Landra thought desperately that perhaps she, too, was lost. Suddenly she saw with greater relief than she had ever felt in her life the tall figure and bright hair of Hollis Freman. He somehow made his way toward her and with his arm around her, supporting her, almost pulling her along, they reached the outside edge of the crowd.

"Hollis," she said, able to breathe easier now in the shady space beneath a small sweet-gum tree, "Hollis, someone shot Adam!"

His eyes were wide with shock. "Is that what happened? I just arrived and saw the mob, but I didn't hear the shot. Who did it?"

"I . . . I don't know . . . they had just come from that office over there," she indicated with a limp little wave of her hand. "Hollis, did you read . . . have you heard what—"

He interrupted. "Yes, I did. It answers a lot of questions, but it raises some, too."

"Those people at Greenlea, they . . . they're *lepers*!" Her voice was strangled, her horror unspeakable.

"That's what I understand. It's been a pretty well-kept secret, though I've been here such a short time I wouldn't have known about it anyway." His eyes were shadowed by drawn brows, and his face wore an expression far more serious than Landra had ever seen.

"And Bethany, my sister . . . she had it, too." Landra buried her face in her hands, unable to bear the bright sunshine, the hot air around her, the still angry buzzing of the crowd. Her knees buckled, and she felt quite faint. "Hollis . . ."

He caught her before she fell. "I'd better get you someplace safer, where you can lie down." As though she weren't five-foot seven and a healthy hundred and twenty-five pounds, he easily swung her up into his arms and began to walk toward the road to his house, having come out on foot. Just then Carrie Chaumont pushed her way out of the crowd, and catching sight of them, hurried over.

"What happened to her?" She glanced over her shoulder anxiously, and bit her lip at the sight of two men, Dr. Dyer and another, as they helped Adam into a carriage, shouting as they did so to the angry crowd who seemed bent on reaching Adam.

"She fainted," said Hollis. "I've got to get her—"

"Bring her this way. I've got a buggy." She led the way to where a horse stood tethered, his head bowed low in the blazing sun. "You're a doctor, aren't you?" she said tersely to Hollis. When he nodded, placing Landra gently on the seat of the buggy, she said, "Then you'd better go and see if there's anything you can do."

"But Landra—"

"I'll see to her; I'll take her to my place. Go on," she urged, "and come back and tell us how he is."

For a moment Hollis stood indecisively, his eyes on Landra's pale face. He guessed, correctly, that she was in a state of shock. "The most important thing is to get her to a cool place, and keep her quiet."

"All right, all right, but please—I have to know if he's hurt badly!" She climbed into the rig beside Landra and with one last anguished look toward Adam, set off smartly, leaving Hollis where he stood.

CHAPTER 10

Carrie Chaumont drove quickly, looking over her shoulder to make sure no one was following them. When they came to her small house, she hurried Landra inside and locked the door with relief.

The shades were drawn against the noon heat, and there was the light, pleasant odor of something cooking drifting in from the kitchen. She steered Landra to a chair and pushed her into it. A little black girl, her eyes wide with curiosity, sat on the shiny linoleum floor with the baby. He looked up and saw Carrie, gave a happy crow, and began crawling rapidly toward her. She picked him up, and covered his face with quick, light kisses. "Did you miss me, baby Rob? Sassie, did he cry any?" she asked the grinning little girl, who was not much older than Jeannette.

"No'm, he didn't cry hardly; he's a good baby. I give him a sugar tit, like Mam does our little 'uns, and he shet right up!" Sassie nodded happily as Carrie pried the grimy, soggy packet from Rob's fat fist. When he protested she changed her mind and let him have it as she put him down on the floor. Landra sat in the chair where she'd been put, like a zombie.

"Sassie, here's the nickle I promised you for looking after Rob. Now you go on home, and . . ." She hesitated. Would the child be more likely to keep her mouth shut about Landra if she warned her, or if she said nothing? She chewed her lip, then said, "Sassie, I like the way you look after the baby. If you won't tell anybody I've got company," she looked pointedly at Landra, "I'll give you ten cents next time you stay with Rob."

Wisely the child looked from Carrie to Landra, and nodded her head. "Sure, Miss Carrie, whatever you says is fine." She

94

flashed a bright, toothy smile, then slipped out the back door.

Carrie took a deep breath and closed her eyes, seeing in her mind's eye Adam's ashen face, the blood . . . She winced, as if it had been her own blood. Dyer would see to him, and that young doctor, Freman, would be there. Fiercely she told herself it was just the same as if it had been her own flesh the bullet ripped through. When you love someone the way she loved Adam, whatever happens to him happens to you. If he was happy, she was, too; and if he hurt . . .

She fought back the bitterness as she looked at Landra. It was pretty plain to her that even though she was his sister-in-law, she'd been nothing but trouble for Adam since she came. Landra had not moved. She sat in the chair with her head against its back, eyes closed. She could have been unconscious. As Carrie studied the tumbled auburn hair, the white, still face with its fine features, she grudgingly allowed that Landra was very beautiful. But that didn't change the fact that she meant trouble for Adam.

Landra moaned and opened her eyes. At the sight of Carrie she frowned and said, "Why did you bring me here?"

Carrie put the baby in his chair and began to prepare his lunch in the tiny kitchen, a mere continuation of the front room where Landra sat. Rob knew what she was doing, and squealed happily, banging his heels on the chair as he watched the small, dark-haired woman. She worked quickly, efficiently, with an economy of motion, and she did not answer Landra's question.

It was not until Carrie finished feeding Rob, wiped his face carefully and lifted him from the high chair that she looked at Landra and spoke very slowly. "I wasn't sure myself why I did it. But I know, now." Her blue eyes were clear and candid. "Not for your sake, that's certain. For the same reason I do anything, lately."

"Adam?"

"Of course. He's got enough on his mind right now, more than one man ought to have to stand. I guess I just didn't want him worried on your account." She paused. Her gaze on Landra was cold and speculative. "You haven't done anything but make problems for him since you came. It wasn't for you, that's certain; it was for him. I only want to help him."

"Help?" whispered Landra bitterly. "How can you say such a thing, with that baby in your arms, standing in the middle of this . . . this *love-nest* that he obviously pays for—" She choked, her teeth clenched in fury.

"Yes, he pays for the house, and for the baby's clothes, and mine, even, sometimes!" Carrie hugged the baby close, and began to pace the length of the small room. "He gives me money for food, and he comes almost every night to see us; even when he's busy he comes two or three times a week!"

"Stop! I can't stand any more!"

Carrie stopped pacing, her face white with emotion. "*You* can't stand anymore? What about me?"

"What do you mean?" asked Landra wildly. "There you stand, holding the baby that should have been my sister's, boasting how you took her husband and drove her to take her own life, and you say what about *you*? I—"

"You're a fool!" cut in Carrie, her voice icy. Landra had risen to her feet but Carrie said, "Sit down. I'm going to tell you a few things."

Landra sat down and put a shaking hand over her eyes. "I don't want to hear anything you've got to say."

"Well, you're going to anyway." She drew the armless rocker to within a few feet from Landra and sat down. The baby's head nestled against her breast, one dark blue eye peeping shyly at Landra. When Carrie spoke again she was calm. "Isn't he a beautiful baby? Do you see how much he looks like me?" Landra made a strangled sound of protest, but Carrie went on as if she hadn't heard it. "And do you see how much he loves me?" She bent her head and kissed the baby.

Landra could stand it no longer. "There's no need to be so cruel! Why must you—"

Carrie broke in calmly. "If that's what it seems like to you, I'm sorry. I just wanted you to realize that I don't *have* to tell the truth, that people would believe Rob is mine if I told them that. Oh, I wish he was!"

Landra stared in confusion at the young woman whose clear blue eyes had filled with tears. "Isn't he your baby?" Carrie shook her head almost violently. "Then whose is he?"

"He's your sister's son. Adam brought him to me the day he was born. I've had him here, and taken care of him, and loved him . . ." She stopped, the tears choking her.

"Adam took Bethany's child and brought him here? That's monstrous! Why would he do such a thing?"

"To save his life!" Carrie said fiercely. "Mrs. Jarrett had . . . she had leprosy. And Adam was afraid the baby would get it; it's very dangerous for babies . . ."

The enormity of Bethany's situation struck Landra then. A victim of one of the most dread diseases known, her newborn infant snatched from her, and Adam . . . "If what you're saying is true, how could you possibly have been so totally inhuman to take her husband, too?"

Carrie recoiled from the anger, the utter revulsion in Landra's voice. "No, I didn't, not once while she was alive did I ever say, or do anything to make him—"

"Love you? Share your bed?" Landra finished coldly. "Surely you don't expect me to believe he comes here night after night, and doesn't take what's so obviously offered to him?"

"That's exactly the truth, whatever you choose to believe. I won't deny I love him; I have from the first day when he came to me and asked if I would take the baby and care for it, before Rob was even born." She kissed the soft dark curls of the little boy, who had fallen asleep.

"Why did he choose you? Rene—Mrs. Chaumont—said you were—" She stopped, but it was too late.

"She doesn't think I'm a 'good' woman, does she?" Carrie smiled grimly. "Well, I'm not. That's the very reason he came to me. If I turned up with a baby and no father, no one would be surprised. 'You know how Carrie always was,' they'd say. 'I always knew she'd get caught,' they'd say." She fixed Landra with her intense blue gaze. "But I've never even looked at another man since he came, and that's the truth. He knows it, too. And after all, there aren't that many people around who'd want to take a child under those circumstances; the baby of a . . . I'm sorry, a leper. I wasn't afraid then, and I'm not now."

"Why aren't you afraid? If it was so dangerous for the baby, surely you aren't all that fearless." Her own reactions when she realized she had spent the previous night with the three of them at Greenlea were suddenly brought back afresh. She found she was unable to speak louder than a whisper. *Is it that . . . that contagious?*"

"Adam says only for infants and young children. An adult doesn't catch it so easily. He says you have to be physically run down, and only at certain stages can a person who's got it pass it to someone else."

"But there are other doctors who disagree with him—"

"Adam knows more than all of them put together!"

"You'll have to admit you're prejudiced," Landra said wearily. "I'm not sure about anything."

Carrie watched her a few moments before she spoke. "There's one thing I'm sure about. When this hospital thing is settled, and Adam doesn't have so much on his mind, I'll be here, and he knows it." She shook her head, eyes closed. "He's driven himself like a crazy man since she died, trying to find a treatment, a cure, something. I only hope he wasn't hurt bad. Oh, dear God, I have to think he wasn't."

Landra agreed. "Yes, we have to believe that. Carrie, I—" She hesitated, unsure as to how to phrase her next statement. "The baby, he's my nephew, and I feel responsible for him. It isn't as though I don't appreciate all you've done for him, I certainly do. You've done more than anyone could expect. But now—"

Carrie's head came up, her eyes blazing; her cheeks flamed with an intensity of feeling that charged her voice. "This baby," she placed a swift, light kiss on his head, "is like my own. He *is* my own! He's never had another mother except me, and I don't intend to give him up. And his father—"

"Yes, Carrie," said Landra, watching her closely, "what about his father? Has he made promises to you, or told you how he feels about you?"

"He has never once, not once, said anything that was not completely, totally honorable to me! And if you think otherwise, you don't know him very well." Her words were quiet, and cold as the grave.

Landra was chastened. "I'm sorry. This thing has been terribly difficult for me; surely you can see that."

"I can see that you only just came, that the rest of us have had to live it," said Carrie with keen perception.

Landra swallowed. "You're right, of course. I'm sorry, Carrie. I misjudged the situation and all of you. Please forgive me." She stood trying to rearrange her hair, smooth her wrinkled dress.

Her defeat, her humiliation was apparent, and Carrie relented. She nodded, then said softly, "Would you like to hold him?"

"I . . . thank you, you're very kind." She took the sleeping baby. After one last, searching look Carrie turned and went into the other room, closing the door softly after her. Landra stared down at Rob, watched as his mouth moved slightly. "Little piggy," she whispered. "Eating even in your sleep . . ."

He was a big, sturdy child, obviously well looked after. She watched him until she could bear it no longer and closed her eyes tightly. He was so beautiful. The image of the deathly quiet nursery at Greenlea came to her mind, and she thought of all the carefully stitched things. The little shirt he wore now was good enough, but not like those others. Bethany must have sat for many painful hours in that empty nursery, making clothes she knew her baby would never wear, staring at the empty crib, feeling the agony of empty arms.

She held Rob all the tighter; then he stirred and opened his eyes. At first he stared at her, knowing she was strange. Then his natural openness asserted itself and he was soon chuckling and crowing at her efforts to amuse him.

A short time later there was a knock at the front door, and when Carrie opened it, there stood a very anxious-looking Hollis.

"Landra!" he exclaimed as he came into the room and straight toward her. "Are you all right?"

"Yes, I'm fine. Look, Hollis, this is Rob, my nephew," she said, trying the words out.

"Nephew? But . . ." Hollis began.

Carrie, her eyes full of worry, interrupted, "For heaven's sake, tell us! Adam, what about Adam?"

"They wouldn't let me do anything, but I hung around long enough to hear that the bullet went through his upper arm. How bad it is, I'm not sure. At least it missed his heart," he said grimly to Carrie.

She closed her eyes at even the thought. "Thank God," she breathed. "Where . . . where have they taken him?"

"To Greenlea; he insisted on it. I'm sure Dr. Delacroix is more than able to take care of him, and the bullet did go through." He turned to Landra. "What do you want to do now?"

"Go to Greenlea, of course," she said, holding the baby tight for a moment; reluctantly she returned him to Carrie. "He's wet, I guess." She smoothed a damp spot on her skirt ruefully.

"I'll take care of him." Carrie's chin was held high, but the look of pain in her eyes betrayed her. "You . . . you'll let me know how Adam is?"

"Yes, Carrie, I will. And Carrie—" She hesitated, then added, "I know you'll take care of Rob, and Adam knows it, too."

Carrie merely nodded, and turned away to hide the bright

shine of tears. "Just . . . have somebody come and tell me about Adam, please."

They left her, both Landra and Hollis quiet, thinking what lay ahead.

CHAPTER 11

The dusk was deepened by low-hanging clouds as they drove down the road to Greenlea. Landra had almost forgotten the peculiar feeling of a summer storm in Louisiana. Somehow it suited her mood now. Occasionally a bright jag of lightning tore the sky and the horse shied at the accompanying boom of thunder. The first few drops began falling on the small buggy, and by the time they reached Greenlea they could barely see the house through the rain. Landra shivered as she tried to find the glow of a lamp, anything. Could she force herself to go inside, knowing what waited? She felt as though too much had happened, that the weight of it all would crush her. The worst fears of her fearful imagination had come to pass. Bethany was dead, lost forever to her and Adam, and to little Rob. Her mind refused to contemplate the pain her sister had had to face, but the underlying horror of it all telegraphed a message to her unwilling mind.

The faceless man with his useless clawed hands; Jimmy, whose eyes were such anguish; and pale, anxious Rose—how had the thing affected her? Quite suddenly Landra realized the possible consequences of the time she'd spent in the dark house with them.

"Hollis . . ." Her voice faltered, and she felt his hand reach for hers. "I'm not sure I have the courage to go in, but I must."

He squeezed her hand tightly. "Not necessarily. In fact, as a doctor, I'd advise against it."

Fear clutched at her stomach. "What do you mean? And what do you know about . . . it?" The word *leprosy* would not come to her tongue. "How contagious do you think it is? Is it possible that I already . . ." She trailed off, appalled at what she was asking. Hadn't Carrie said it wasn't contagious, except under certain circumstances? She wished she could see his face better; wished she could gauge his reaction.

He hesitated, then said, "You deserve honesty, Landra. I only wish I were better equipped to inform you. I'm just not sure. There are two diametrically opposed schools of thought about how leprosy is carried, and whether or not it's virulently contagious. Some of the fellows at the University believe—"

"But what do *you* believe, Hollis?" Landra felt as though she were drowning in a sea of fear and unknown terrors.

He shook his head. "Landra, I wish I knew. I've never been faced with the reality of the disease. Of course, we discussed it during the course on tropical diseases, but it was just that, only theoretical discussion. Most doctors never come across it in actual practice unless they go to some of the countries where it's endemic, like some of the islands or Africa."

"Cuba."

"What?" Startled, Hollis shot a puzzled look at Landra.

"The faceless man fought in the war in Cuba. I thought Rose meant he was injured in a battle, but she obviously meant he had contracted it there. But what about my sister, who was never away from this country?" Suddenly Landra was overwhelmed by the enormity, the hopelessness of it all. "Oh, Hollis, I don't think I can bear it—there's no hope, none of us have any hope!" She turned toward him, but she did not cry. There were no more tears, not in the depth of despair she felt now.

"There, there, Landra," he said as he would to a frightened child, "you're wrong. There is hope. For Rose, and that young man you cared for in the night, for Dr. Jarrett, even that poor man who has been all but ruined by this thing. There is hope."

Landra raised her head, the anger strong in her again. "How can you say that? Perhaps it's because you've not seen it, as I have, because you've not had someone die of it, as I have! If you had, you couldn't say there's hope!"

Hollis hesitated, as though he were about to say something and doubted if he should. Then, searching Landra's eyes in the dimness, he said, very slowly, "What about God, Landra? What part does He have in all this?"

Almost hysterically she cried, "That's exactly what I've been wondering! Just where is God, anyway, and where was He when my sister gave up her newborn baby, and where was He last night while that poor boy cried out in such pain I thought I'd die with it myself. *Where is God?* And what does He think of that man whose body is rotting . . . *rotting* away?" She did not cry, but her body was shaking so with the depth of her feelings that he put his hands on her shoulders and held them tightly, as though by the very strength of his will, he could quiet the shuddering spasms. Finally she was still, but the stillness held even more significance than her violent emotion; she was totally empty now, without defenses.

His voice was soft beside her as he slowly asked, "Landra, do you remember when I told you how I felt when I came up from the river when I was baptized?" She nodded her head almost imperceptibly. "Do you remember how you felt when you were baptized?" Again, a small, tired nod. "Was it the same for you . . . answer honestly; it's very important."

A long moment passed before she drew away slightly, her head low. "I . . . no, it wasn't. I was pleased, but . . . but it was because my father was so happy. He wanted it for me, and I would have done anything—"

"I thought perhaps that was the case. Oh, not then," he hastened to add. "I was like most youngsters, only concerned with myself. But yesterday, and tonight when you were so disturbed, I began to wonder whether or not we had . . . have the same relationship with Christ." His tone was gentle, with no hint of self-righteousness or accusation.

"What do you mean?" The words were barely audible, almost pained; she didn't dare to hope that he had answers she did not yet understand.

"Landra, I'm not a minister, and I'm not theologically learned. But I have an absolute assurance of the love of God in my heart." A little sigh escaped her lips, and he knew she had no such assurance. He tipped her chin up. "That assurance of God's love is what you need."

"But how can I have that assurance when things are so horrible, when all I can see is the total unfairness, the pain and agony, and God doesn't seem to even care, much less love us!"

"Faith, Landra," he said simply. "Faith to believe that no matter how bad things are, God's hand is in it all, that ultimately we'll be able to see it. And we have to believe that God does not *make* these things happen. I suspect you wonder."

Landra was nothing, if not honest. "Yes, I do," she whispered.

He nodded. "Don't feel badly; many people wonder the same thing. I have myself, especially when, as a doctor, I've seen such things as those poor souls have to face, suffering that seems so grossly unfair. But I searched the Scriptures, and asked Him to guide me. One of my answers was a verse in James. It says, 'Every good gift and every perfect gift is from above, and cometh down from the Father of lights, with whom is no variableness, neither shadow of turning.' Don't you see, Landra, there is no darkness in Him, only light, only goodness. This thing, this awful disease, is not of God."

A sudden memory assailed Landra. "The other day, just before Adam was shot, a woman in the crowd shouted at me, saying that leprosy is a punishment from God. That's not so, it's not so! My sister did nothing to deserve a punishment like that."

"You're right, you're right," he said soothingly. "And God did not cause the others, those in Adam's care, to become ill with it as a punishment or for any other reason; I'm sure of that. And there's something else I'm sure of."

"What?" The word was pitifully small.

"That He stands ready to help, to comfort, to be with us no matter how terrible the problems we face. Do you remember what it said in the verse from James, about good and perfect gifts?"

"Yes."

"What is God's best and most perfect gift?" He answered himself, feeling that her heart was ready, that she wanted to hear. "It's love, Landra, love. Without it we are all destitute. And the most important way God showed His love for us is in another gift, His Son Jesus. 'For God so loved the world, that he gave his only begotten Son, that whosoever believeth in him should not perish, but have everlasting life.' "

"John 3:16," she said faintly.

"Yes. The verse we all learned, the one we all can quote, the one most vital. Landra," he said urgently, "do you believe, do you believe that it was for you that God gave His Son, that Jesus gave His life?"

Landra found herself in a peculiar state; she felt light, almost as though she were weightless, floating above herself. But there was a clarity in her mind and she knew the words, familiar though they were, were new. Her eyes were tightly closed, and she breathed deeply, bringing air into her body and the realization of the truth Hollis had spoken into her mind. It was for her. God's most precious, good gift, His Son . . . given for her. "Yes," she breathed, "I do believe. Oh, Hollis, I do!" Tears flowed quietly down her face, unnoticed and unheeded.

Neither of them spoke for many moments, and when Hollis did, his head was low, his voice awed. "Oh, Lord, thank you for this, thank you for coming into Landra's heart and mind."

"Yes," she whispered, "I thank you, too." She buried her face in his shoulder, and he held her gently, thinking only of the joy. They sat there for a long, long while. Finally she straightened, and pulled away. "I have to go in, I know that. But Hollis, it's very strange—"

"What?" he said, wishing he could see her face in the gloom.

"Well, I'm not sure I can explain. Everything in there is the same . . . poor Adam is hurt, no telling how badly, those three are still desperately ill, but somehow—" She stopped, unable after all to voice her feelings.

Hollis did it for her. "Everything is the same, but you. You're different, Landra, and you will never be the same."

She smiled for the first time in a long while. "That's good. I've always tried so hard to . . . to be good, but Hollis, there were a lot of times when I didn't like myself."

Warmly he said, "I can't imagine not liking you, but I think I understand. He was quiet for a moment, then said, "Landra, are you sure you want to go in there?"

"I'm sure. Besides," she added, her voice soft, "I'm not going in alone."

"You want me to go in with you? Of course I will."

She shook her head. "That's not what I meant. *He's* with me, Hollis, and that means I do have something to offer them now. I didn't before, you know. I tried so hard with Jimmy, and I was such a failure."

"That's because you had nothing but your own strength to give. None of us are strong enough in ourselves, Landra."

"I thought I was, and never have I been proved so wrong. But it'll be different now." She made a move to get down from the buggy.

"I'll walk you to the door." Hollis sprang down, and went round to lift her down. For just a second he held her close, then released her. "Oh, Landra, I love you," he said softly.

She smiled brilliantly up at him. "I love you too, and—" She glanced toward the house, then added, wonder in her voice, "And I love *them*."

Hollis nodded slowly; he seemed about to say something, then just took her arm and together they ran through the rain to the veranda.

The slender panels on either side of the door were dark, and Landra could not see into the blackness of the house. Finally, after almost a minute she saw a faint glimmer, then Rose, her face illuminated by the lamp she carried, came into view. Her brown hair hung loose and she wore a dark dress, so all they could see was the white, pale face floating in the slowly moving lamplight. She was moving so slowly.

"Who is that?" asked Hollis, his voice hushed.

"She's Rose, one of Adam's patients," Landra said. "There are three of them. You met her the other day, remember?"

"Oh." Just one small word, but Landra heard in it the shared anguish, the pity.

The door swung open then and Landra said, "Don't be afraid, Rose, it's just me, and Dr. Freman."

Rose lifted the lamp higher and peered at Hollis. "Yes, I see. but I'm not supposed to let him in . . . Dr. Delacroix is out looking for you—"

At that moment they heard a buggy drive up. Lucas Delacroix leaped out and ran through the pouring rain onto the veranda, brushing the water from his jacket.

"Miss Cole! I've been looking all over. Where were you?"

"At Carrie Chaumont's."

He stopped his careful brushing and stared at her. "It never occurred to me to look there. I'd have thought she'd—" He turned to Hollis. "What are you doing here?" he asked coldly.

"I brought Miss Cole home," replied Hollis, undaunted by Lucas' tone.

"Well, until after the council meets, I'll have to ask you to stay away from Greenlea. Do you understand, Freman?"

Hollis ignored him and said to Landra, his hand on her arm, "Come back with me, Landra, please. You know the Chaumonts would welcome you."

She looked into the darkness beyond the light of the lamp which Rose held. Somewhere in the house were Jimmy and that other man, whose name she didn't even know. There was no reason whatever for her to stay in this terrible, dark house, every reason for her to leave with the young man whose fingers were grasping her arm urgently.

She placed her own cold fingers on his and said slowly, "No, Hollis, I can't go with you; I have to stay. But will you come back tomorrow?" she asked, glancing defiantly at Dr. Delacroix. It was one thing to make a decision as she just had, another to foolishly close all doors.

"Of course, if you're sure that's what you want." He looked at her steadily. "I don't really want to leave you here, but I think I understand."

"I'll be all right. Good night, Hollis, and thank you for bringing me home."

"Tomorrow, I'll see you tomorrow," he said with one last frowning glance at the silent Lucas. "And remember, you're not alone now . . ."

The three of them watched as he left; it was Lucas who uttered a stifled oath. "That one means trouble."

"He's been very kind to me, Dr. Delacroix."

"Bethany—Mrs. Jarrett—called me Lucas; you can too. Let's go inside," he said gruffly.

She followed him in. The only light within the house came from the lamp which Rose held. Landra's eyes met the girl's for a brief second; she saw the pain and shame in them, knew Rose was aware that Landra had found out what plagued them all. Landra wanted to say something to reassure her, but Rose placed the lamp on a table in the hall, then softly disappeared, walking into the darkness which led to the kitchen.

"Why doesn't she light more lamps?"

"That should be obvious—you saw that mob today. If they should decide their righteous indignation is stronger than their blasted superstitious fear, it could go badly for us. Better that they don't see lights, should one find the courage to snoop." He paused, peered in the direction Rose had gone, and said, "Besides, these days Rose has the idea she should get about in the darkness as much as possible."

"But why?"

"Because of Jimmy. She feels if she can experience what he's going to have to face—and very soon, I'm afraid—she can understand better how to help him."

"He's going blind, isn't he?" Landra asked.

He nodded. "Yes." One word, awful in its implications.

"Is it part of . . . of the—"

"Leprosy?" Lucas supplied. "Hard to say that ugly word the

first few times, isn't it? Yes, it's a condition called photophobia, an extreme sensitivity to light. The pain is an unbelievable torture; but when the thing runs it course and he's totally blind, ironically enough there'll be no more pain." He stood by the curving staircase, one smartly booted foot on the bottom step.

Landra tried to see his face more clearly in the dim lamp-light. "Lucas, how is Adam? Is he hurt badly?" Her voice shook a little, for it was almost as cold in the house as it had been outside, despite the fact it was May. The rain had thoroughly drenched her clothing.

"You're cold," he said shortly. "I can hear your teeth chattering. One thing we don't need at this point is someone else to take care of." He picked up the lamp, took her arm, then gently but firmly led her up the stairs into her room. He placed the lamp as far from the window as possible and turned the wick low.

He started to leave without speaking again, but Landra said, "You didn't answer my question about Adam, Lucas."

He looked at her for a long moment, then closed his eyes; he rubbed the spot between them with the tips of his fingers. "It isn't as bad as it could have been, that's certain."

"When may I see him?"

"He told me to bring you as soon as you got here."

"He knew I was coming? How could he?"

Lucas shrugged. "He said you never stayed out of anything when you could jump in the middle of it. I gather you're rather impetuous," he added dryly.

"Then may I see him now? Lucas, is he going to be all right?"

"The bullet didn't hit a bone, thank God, but there was some muscle damage, and I had a terrible time stopping the bleeding. I was worried for a while." He stopped, then added, "I feel he needs rest more than he needs to be disturbed, at least until morning. And you, Landra Cole, are a most disturbing young woman." She met his steady gaze, and was not surprised when he went on. "She was just the opposite. Whenever she came into the room, you felt the peace and serenity come in, too. She could smile, and you felt calm and good."

"Bethany."

He didn't answer as he turned to go. Just as he was closing the door, she ran to it with the lamp. "Here, won't you need this?" The hall outside was in dense darkness now; the stairs were not even visible. "I'm afraid you'll fall. There's probably a candle here in the room. You take this."

With the lamp close to his face, she saw the pain in his eyes as he answered, "No, you keep it. Since she's gone, it's all pretty much the same, daylight or dark. Like Jimmy, I'll have to learn to make my way without light." Then, as though he were ashamed for being so melodramatic, he pulled the door shut, leaving Landra holding the lamp.

His slow, steady footsteps faded, and she stood in the small room which seemed to grow smaller as the conflict in her mind grew larger. Lucas had said she should wait until morning to see Adam, that he had been very concerned about not being able to stop the bleeding right away. She clasped her hands and pressed them against her mouth, hard. She had felt so light, so buoyant outside in the carriage with Hollis. And now, in this house where no one dared to light a lamp, where the cold chilled her to the marrow, she felt fear, and a terrible sense of foreboding.

With shaking fingers she undid the buttons of her dress and hung it, glad to be rid of the clammy dampness. She slipped into a nightgown and got into bed, pulling the covers up over her ears. There was a long-forgotten odor about them, the smell of the hard-fought battle between her mother and mildew. The battle was lost forever now, and mustiness almost choked her before she could pull the quilt down and tuck it firmly under her chin.

She tried to sleep. With her eyes closed she lay rigid until she could bear it no longer and slipped from the bed to her knees and clasped her hands tightly.

"Father—" Landra stopped, quite suddenly, wonderfully aware deep within herself that for the first time she could really use that name now, that it was true in a way it had never been before. For a long while she was very still, lost in the thought of her Father's love. She found that even the loss of her parents was somehow easier to bear; the heavenly Father was near and loved her. Then, a little smile curving her mouth, she began to pray softly, a prayer of thankfulness, of asking for help in the grave situation all around her; and finally a prayer of praise from her heart which was beginning to know God in a new, exciting way.

When she rose, light and free again, Landra started to slip beneath the musty covers, then stood indecisively for a moment. She reached for her soft challis wrapper on the back of the room's only chair and drew it on. Thinking that she would just look in on Adam to reassure herself about his condition, she crept down the hall to his door. It was ajar, and she pushed it open very quietly, expecting to find him asleep.

"Come in, Landra," he said, his voice betraying his weakness. "I wondered when you'd come."

There was a small lamp with its wick turned low on his bedside table; even in the dimness the extreme pallor of his face was evident. He struggled to sit up and she went to help, propping a pillow behind his back. Beneath the white fabric of his long, white nightshirt the bulky outline of his bandaged arm showed, the empty sleeve hanging loose. She had thought she was prepared, but the shock of seeing him so helpless was worse than she'd imagined. "Oh, Adam, are you—is it very bad?"

He shrugged. "Could have been worse," he said laconically. "You were there, I take it?"

"Yes, I had gone to town to . . . to find out the truth about things. Someone handed me a newspaper, and I'd just read that story about your hospital." She halted, then whispered, "It was like a nightmare, a horrible nightmare."

A spasm of pain twisted his face, and he put his free hand on the injured arm. "That's certainly true. I'm glad you weren't hurt, and I'm sorry you had to find out about things that way."

Suddenly the whole scene—the mob, the newspaper article, and her own stunned, shocked reaction—rushed back. "Oh, Adam, I can't bear to think of what Bethany must have suffered! And she loved you so! From the first all she ever wanted to do was make you happy, and you lied to me. You said she died of pneumonia. Why didn't you tell me the truth?"

His face was unbearably bleak. "It was the truth. She did die of pneumonia."

"Are you trying to tell me she didn't have leprosy?"

"No, she had it." He shifted his weight on the bed, and winced as he placed the injured arm at a better angle. His eyes were not on Landra; he was staring at the dark window. She could see the small reflections of them both in each of the panes. When he spoke again the words were slow, and infinitely weary. "But people rarely die of Hansen's disease itself—almost always of something else. In Bethany's case it was pneumonia."

Even though she knew it was bad for him, that it would probably upset him further, Landra was compelled to say, "But she did . . . what she did because of her sickness, and because you took the baby away."

"I had to!"

"And those three patients downstairs, did you bring them here because you had to?"

"Yes, they had nowhere to go, and I'd hoped to help them."

"At the expense of your own wife?" Landra cried as she stood up in agitation. "Oh, Adam, how could you do such a thing? How could you justify putting your work ahead of Bethany? No matter how important you believed it was."

He stared incredulously at her. "That's why you're so angry—you actually believed I was responsible for Bethany's contracting Hansen's disease!"

"Well, weren't you?" Her tone was demanding, but she felt the slow, painful beginning of doubt steal into her mind. "Didn't you bring them here?"

The look on his face frightened her. "Yes, I brought them here. But only after Bethany's illness had been diagnosed, and only because she agreed it was the thing to do!" He stared at her whitened face, then said slowly, "Did you really believe that of me . . . did you, Landra?"

"Adam, I . . . I don't know what to say. You acted so strange that first day I came to Greenlea, and you refused to tell me about Bethany. If you'd just told me."

"I'm really sorry, Landra, but I couldn't. I wanted to; you had every right to know. But I couldn't."

"But why not? It would have saved us from so much." Her hands twisted in her lap, seemingly of their own accord. "Please, I still don't understand."

He took a deep, painful breath before he spoke. "She was consumed with the shame of being a . . . leper. It became the most important thing in her life, that no one know she had Hansen's disease. Absolutely everything had been taken from her, the child, and—" He halted, then faced Landra, his eyes darker than ever. "I promised her. It was a matter of honor. Considering what you thought of me, I suppose you find that hard to believe, but it's true."

Stunned by the awesome implications of his words, Landra stared at him for a timeless moment. "Adam, I'm so sorry. Can you forgive me?"

He nodded, and the silence deepened again. Finally he said, "I loved her so."

"I know you did." She saw the total exhaustion on his ashen face, and rose to stand beside his bed. "Adam, the important thing now is for you to recover from this." She touched his arm gently. They both were aware that he would never completely recover from the pain of losing Bethany. A fleeting thought of sympathy flickered through her mind: Carrie Chaumont's hopes certainly looked futile. The man lying here would never be free to love a woman again. He had given himself too totally in life, and Bethany's death had not freed him. "There's one more thing." She stopped, then said, "Perhaps I should wait until tomorrow."

A tiny ghost of a smile flitted across his fine features. "Landra, you may look mature and adult, but you're the same. Speak first, think later . . . what is it?"

"I think you're being unfair about Dr. Freman. He's really a fine young man, and he wants to help."

Adam's face grew stern, with no hint of a smile now. "You're wrong there, Landra. I have it on good authority that the opposition needs support; he's a prime candidate."

She frowned. "What do you mean?"

"I mean he's very new in the community, and he needs a foothold. This could very well be what he needs, a chance to land himself in good with the other doctors, the ones who are—" A sudden paroxysm of coughing shook his body, and before Landra could do anything Dr. Delacroix came into the room.

"Miss Cole," he said even as he helped Adam to sit upright and was feeling for his pulse, "I thought I advised against your coming in here tonight." He was supporting Adam's shoulders with one hand. "Slow your breathing, Adam, think, slow . . ."

Landra started to reply, then decided it was better to just slip out and back to her own room. There was no question of sleep now. Landra took her purse and went to sit on the window seat, putting the lamp on the sill. She had the even dozen letters spread out beside her before she remembered Lucas' warning about lights in the windows. Hastily she moved the lamp to the bedside table. The soft glow of lamplight shone on the last correspondence between her and her sister.

She carefully arranged Bethany's in proper sequence, according to date, then placed hers beside them. Each in turn was so inconsistent and incongruous as the last, the one that had brought her here. As she looked closely at it, she could see what had not been so obvious before. The handwriting was, with each succeeding letter, less like Bethany's neat, ladylike script, and

Landra could only imagine her sister's reasoning. How could she have hoped to deceive them indefinitely?

It was quite possible, although Landra shrank from such a possibility, that Bethany had been in the grip of a desperate madness. She dropped the letter, finally realizing now what Bethany had had to face, and why she had been unable to go on. Without her beauty or health, without her family, or her precious baby, what was left to her? Nothing, absolutely nothing.

After gathering up the letters carefully and putting them away, she lay down once more. The lamp was almost out of oil, so she blew it out. *Leprosy*. In the dark she faced the word, trying to remember anything she'd ever heard about it, which was precious little—and horrible. Oh, Bethany! The pain of the loss of her sister filled her until she thought she'd burst. The tears ran down the sides of her face and dampened her hair, but she did not notice or wipe them away. There were no words, even in prayer, that could ease the pain. She moaned softly. "Oh, God, dear Father . . . please help me. . . ."

After a while the pain relented; she closed her eyes, and in the early hours of the morning she slept.

CHAPTER 12

It was midmorning before Landra hesitantly approached the laboratory. She stood outside the door for several moments, then knocked, somehow unwilling to face Adam, but knowing she must.

"Come in," she heard Adam call out.

That odor assailed her once more as she entered. It was heavy, pervading, and decidedly unpleasant. Adam stood behind the long table, his white lab coat draped over the sling which held his bandaged arm close to his side. He was still quite pale, and there were dark shadows under his eyes. His hair was combed a little carelessly, and he did not smile as he tried clumsily to pour the contents of a beaker into a small vial, spilling a trickle. His right arm was in the sling, and his left served him poorly.

Landra went to him and took the beaker. The offensive odor was overpowering, and she grimaced. "Here, let me help you. What is that awful stuff?"

"Chaulmoogra oil."

"But what *is* it?" she persisted. "Is it the treament Rose mentioned? For the . . . leprosy?"

"Hansen's disease," he said shortly. "Call it Hansen's disease. It's caused by a microbe first identified by a Norwegian scientist named Gerhard Hansen, in 1874. If we could eliminate the word leprosy, and all it stands for—" He stopped, then went on slowly. "People react insanely to the very word. But then, you saw that for yourself yesterday, didn't you?" He glanced down at his arm.

"I certainly did. You're up; does that mean your arm is better or that you're the same, too? Stubborn, I mean."

114

He gave her a keen look that said he knew exactly what she was talking about. Her mother Marie had commented many times on the fact that both Landra and Adam showed amazingly similar characteristics, stubbornness among them. He rewarded her with a little smile. "Both, I guess. I'm better, and I couldn't stand being on my back another minute." He rummaged in a small drawer until he found a cork which he put into the vial of heavy yellow liquid. "This awful smelling stuff, as you call it, is only one of the multitudes of treatments we try, with no assurance of appreciable, ultimate results. There's a legend about the discovery of the therapeutic value of the chaulmoogra plant."

Landra saw that his attention was not really on her now. His voice was low, almost hypnotic, as he related the tale of how a Burmese prince stricken with leprosy went alone into the jungle to contemplate the evils of the world, how he was instructed in a vision to eat the seeds of a certain tree, and was cured. Because of Adam's seeming unawareness of her, Landra was able to watch him closely; the square, earnest, black-browed face, the tall, broad body, slightly stooped in the long white coat . . . for a few moments she could see the Adam she remembered.

". . . historically, however, it wasn't until 1853 that Dr. F. J. Mowat, a British Civil surgeon on the west coast of India, mentioned chaulmoogra oil as a treatment. Unfortunately, it's more effective on Asians than Caucasians. We keep trying." He looked at her with his full attention now. "I suppose you saw the man with me yesterday?"

"Dr. Dyer?"

He nodded. "Dyer was responsible for introducing chaulmoogra oil as a treatment into this country two years ago. He's a brilliant man, and I'm proud to be associated with him," Adam said. "He was a great help with Bethany."

Remembering the first time she'd entered Bethany's room, and the odor of what she now knew was chaulmoogra oil, she asked, "And he treated her with that"—she pointed to the vial she'd helped him fill—"that ridiculous remedy from an occult vision?" She was suddenly quite angry, and all her good intentions fled. "You're supposed to be a scientist; was there nothing else you could do for her? Is that the best your fine scientific knowledge could offer?"

"We did what we could! If you only knew some of the so-called 'cures' and remedies even reputable doctors use, usually out of desperation. One favorite among Mexican patients is herbs steeped in kerosene, and even in the history of official experimentation there are such unlikely things as using anthrax vaccine, colchicine, snake venom, oxygen, plasma, and recently, horse serum."

"Experimentation! Did you experiment with Bethany's treatment? Lucas said all you cared about was your work—"

"If Lucas said that he is a liar," he broke in wearily. "Yes, we tried different treatments, chaulmoogra oil among them. She didn't respond well to it. There are many ways we use it— rubbed into the skin, given orally, and in injections. We'd heard that if it was injected directly into the nodules they'd go away. But it also causes—" He stopped, not meeting her eyes.

"What, Adam?"

"The injections sometimes cause ulcerations of the skin," he answered dully.

A memory flashed briefly through Landra's mind. Bethany was sixteen, and she, Landra, was an envious, flat-chested ten. She had burst into Bethany's room at bedtime to find her tall, slender sister standing before the mirror, night shift in hand. Landra could see, in her mind's eye, the white smoothness of Bethany's body before she had modestly pulled the shift over her head.

Smooth, white, and unblemished—until the monstrous thing had infected her, and then, to think of those injections making ugly ulcers on that body . . . Landra gave a little cry—for Bethany, for Adam, for herself. "Oh, Adam!" She stared at him, seeing her misery reflected in his eyes. "When did you first know, I mean, how can you tell if someone has it?"

Adam said slowly, "There are several ways it manifests itself." He shook his head, as if it needed clearing. When he began to speak again, it was in a detached, almost clinical tone, perhaps because if he spoke generally they would not remember he was describing the symptoms that had been Bethany's. "Sometimes at first the victim suffers from a morning facial puffiness and redness, and the eyes are swollen. A reddish-brown spot appears somewhere, and grows darker and bigger. And the disease often affects the cornea, the eyes."

"Like Jimmy?"

"Yes, like Jimmy. And as in the case of Anson, sometimes it seems to go wild, and the ways it attacks are too horrible to contemplate."

"Is he the other man who is staying here? The one whose face and hands are so . . . so . . ."

"Mutilated?" Adam supplied. "Yes, I'm afraid all we've tried to do has had little or no effect on poor Anson. He comes from a wealthy family and has taken elaborate pains to convince them he is dead."

She recoiled at the thought. "But why? Isn't there something they could do for him? It seems terrible that he should have to suffer both from the disease and alienation from his family. Why?" she repeated.

"He wanted to spare them the inevitable social damage that would occur if it were known he has Hansen's disease."

"Social damage? Adam, surely you can't be serious. Do you mean they wouldn't be invited to the best parties, and they would be socially outcast? That seems to be a small enough price to pay for being a family, for loyalty!"

"That's not what I mean at all. When I said socially, I meant Anson dePaul's father would, in all likelihood, lose a business that has taken three generations to build, and his family would suffer complete ostracism, even as he does now." His voice was deep with controlled anger. "The patients who have the courage to admit themselves to the sanitarium at Indian Camp are, in effect, exiles. They discard their pasts like old clothes—their identities, their loved ones, everything they hold dear."

"But that's terrible!" whispered Landra.

Adam sighed deeply. "Yes, it's terrible. If we could only educate the public, if we could establish the hospital at Elkhorn and give the researchers at the University a chance, we might be able to offer some hope."

"Rose, and Jimmy and Anson—is there hope for them?"

He was quiet for several moments before he spoke. "Rose, perhaps, can be helped. She is like Bethany in the early symptoms she shows. If Bethany had fought it . . ." He ran his free hand through the thick, unruly black hair. "I'm afraid nothing can be done to arrest Jimmy's blindness. And Anson has showed an alarming inability to fight the disease. It seems to be attacking him in almost every way. There is severe throat involvement. The nodules are so numerous in his throat he has difficulty breathing at times, and has resulted in that peculiar voice quality. I'm very much afraid he will need a tracheotomy at any time."

Unwillingly Landra asked, "What is a tracheotomy?"

"It's an emergency operation in which the surgeon cuts through the front of the neck and inserts a tube in the windpipe. If it's not done when indicated, the patient will choke to death. Not only is Anson faced daily with that prospect, he is also plagued by the fact that the bacillus does something—unfortunately we're not sure what—to the calcium balance in the body. I suppose you've heard the grisly tales of lepers' fingers falling off in the soup, or some such horrible thing?"

"Oh, Adam!" Landra shrank back at his words. "Surely that isn't so?"

"No, of course it isn't!" His face was hard, frighteningly bleak. "But it's typical of the drivel people choose to believe, while they ignore the real truths we've managed to uncover. Their fingers and toes don't fall off; the bone cells in them are gradually absorbed and not replaced by new ones as rapidly as they should be. The bones become porous and fragile, and subject to chipping and splitting."

"Is this one of Anson dePaul's problems, as well as the thing about his breathing?"

He nodded. "There's frequently a loss of sensation in affected areas, a sort of anaesthesia, and the patient unknowingly increases damage by submitting his hands and feet to abuses that a well person would avoid because of the pain he would normally feel."

She said slowly, "So that's why Jimmy couldn't wring out the hot cloths for himself, because of the danger of burning himself and not even knowing it. Could his hands become like Mr. dePaul's?" When Adam nodded again she said, "That's . . . that's horrible."

"It's only the beginning. There's the constant possibility of gangrene. Anson is also the victim of massive infiltration of Hansen's bacilli in his face, which has caused the ruin that horrified you so. Sometimes it gives a leonine appearance, because of the thickening and furrowing of the brows and facial structure. It distorts the ear lobes and causes eyebrows to fall out. It can cause destruction of the nerves and bring motor paralysis and the contracting of some muscles, which results in hammer toes and claw hands—"

"Stop!" cried Landra. "I can't stand any more, at least not now . . ." She stared at him in new horror. "Adam, was Bethany like . . . did she have any of those symptoms?"

He did not meet her eyes. "I don't want to talk about it any more than you'd want to hear it. I want . . . I want to forget; if only I could forget." His last words were little more than a groan. Then, with a visible effort he straightened and said, "Landra, I want to ask something of you."

"What?"

"I want—I need you to remain here at Greenlea."

"Of course I will, Adam, as long as you want." Landra was glad for a chance to make up for her earlier skepticism, and waited for him to continue.

But he wasn't looking at her; he had half-turned away, his attention on some papers he had picked up from the counter. "My notes," he explained. "I'll need them for the council meeting on Tuesday. Lucas, at least, had the presence of mind to realize that it would be extremely damaging if you were not present. We must have every shred of support possible. It'll be close, too close, I'm afraid."

"What exactly are you talking about, Adam?"

He met her puzzled gaze, then, and she was aware of a determined, fierce gleam in his black eyes. "Why, the council meeting to decide the fate of Elkhorn, of course. I thought you knew . . . I just assumed—"

"Don't assume anything, please; just explain the situation," she said abruptly, wishing suddenly she were not quite so much Landra at the moment, and little more like Bethany—patient and diplomatic. But she wasn't.

"All right. I've been working with Dyer and some others to bring the hospital for the treatment, and hopefully, the cure for Hansen's disease, nearer to the University at Tulane. Conditions at the existing facility at Indian Camp are intolerable. Elkhorn is an ideal site, and the negotiations for its purchase were completed, and, I thought, approved."

"But not by everyone," put in Landra, thinking of the people in Noirville the day before.

"No. I'm afraid there are a great many people, who, because of their ignorant, superstitious fears, could ruin the whole project." He scowled. "Because of the adverse publicity of a few very biased newspapers, public opposition is so great there's a grave danger we won't be allowed to carry out the plans for establishing the hospital at Elkhorn, and we must!"

"But, Adam, if you've already secured the property, what can they do?"

He put a hand to the back of his neck and rubbed hard, as

if it ached. Finally he said, "When people are whipped to a frenzy, as they were yesterday, it's anybody's guess what they'll do. The Board of Control is gravely concerned. Both sides will have a chance to express their views at that council meeting, and have a fair hearing. I can only hope we'll be able to convince them we're right."

Landra stared at him. "Adam, I've been wondering; in the newspaper article it stated that three of the patients were from a pesthouse—"

"Don't call it that! That's what we're fighting!"

She answered quietly, "That's what *you're* fighting, Adam. I'm just trying to understand the situation. Were any of those three Rose, or Jimmy, or . . . Anson dePaul?"

He nodded. "Anson was a patient there. Dyer has been treating him since the others were taken to Indian Camp, and it was necessary for him to hide like a common criminal when he decided he wouldn't go. Jimmy and Rose were diagnosed by Dr. Dyer, so he felt a responsibility for all three of them. We felt it was unwise, for entirely different reasons, for them to go to Indian Camp. I'm afraid we've placed all our hopes on the new hospital at Elkhorn."

Such a look of sadness crept over his face that Landra caught her lip in her teeth. "Why would it be so bad at Indian Camp for them?"

"I'm sure Rose will explain if you'll ask her. As for Anson, he's all too aware that he could die very soon, and he wanted to be as near his family as possible. They live in New Orleans and sometimes I take him in a covered carriage past his house so he can catch a glimpse of his wife or his daughter. They believe he's dead; have for the past three years." He wasn't looking at Landra when he added, "The poor wretch has so little left to him, how could I deny him shelter? There are two things keeping him going: being near his family, and his book."

"What book?"

"He's trying desperately to get his experiences on paper, to be published after his death under an assumed name. He feels if he can enlighten people about Hansen's disease, it would be his contribution. I understand why it's important to him, why he feels a compulsion to do it. He's an admirable man."

"Did you know him before he contracted the disease?"

"No. He was on the staff at Tulane University with Dyer."

"What did he teach?" asked Landra, feeling compelled to

know more about the man. "And how can he write with his hands the way they are?"

"He was professor of philosophy, and Rose does the actual writing as he dictates to her." Adam looked at her closely. "You find Anson interesting, don't you? Are you still afraid of him?"

Landra hesitated, finding it difficult to verbalize her feelings toward Anson dePaul. Lucas burst into the laboratory before she could answer, his hair blown wildly, the silk handkerchief at his throat awry. "Adam, Dr. Jarrett, they're here!"

Adam forgot Landra. "Who, man, who are you talking about? Is it some of those fools from town? Are they after Jimmy and Anson? Get them at once, we must hide them—"

"No, no," interrupted Lucas. "I'm sorry, you misunderstood me. It's Dr. Dyer and some of the others from the Board who are on our side. They've come to discuss our strategy for the meeting on Tuesday." He was watching Adam closely, as was Landra. Adam's hand was grasping his chin, and his eyes were staring at the corner of the long, white room. It was obvious he had shifted the gears of his mind yet again, and was now already concentrating on the matter at hand.

"Show them in here, Lucas. I have my notes and all the material at hand. Yes, it's better that we talk here." Lucas hurried out, and Adam strode about the room, collecting papers and scowling, trying to stack them one-handed.

Landra went to him, saying, "Here, let me help you." He allowed her to take the notes from him, and she felt that for almost the first time since she'd entered the room, perhaps even since she'd first seen him the other day, he was really aware of her. For a long moment their eyes met. Slowly she squared the papers, being unduly careful to make the corners line up. His tie was undone, and Landra saw with a small pang that there was a spot in one corner. If it was tied properly, perhaps it wouldn't show . . .

She laid the papers down and reached up, saying, "You've a spot on your tie. I'll do it up so it won't show. Your distinguished colleagues will think no one looks after you."

He started to object, and raised his good hand to do it for himself.

In midair her hand stopped as she saw the look of pain. How often Bethany had straightened his tie, had gently teased him about his lack of concern for his appearance. The loss of Bethany would haunt them both for a long time to come. Landra wished she could share her new faith with him, share its comfort. She knew instinctively that now was not the time, but she also was certain God would allow her to if she was willing. "Oh, Adam," she said softly, "I can imagine how hard it's been for you, how you must miss her . . . I do, too."

He nodded, his eyes bleak. "I keep telling myself it will get better, easier, but it doesn't."

She started to speak, to assure him it would, then said nothing, just laid her hand gently on the side of his face for an instant; in her heart she vowed to be a quiet, constant help to him, and finally, a living witness. Deftly she tied his tie, as she had for her father so many times. Just as she finished they heard quick footsteps in the hall, and Lucas burst through the door, followed by several men.

Dr. Isodore Dyer, as imposing a figure in person as he was from a distance or staring at her from the front page of a newspaper, looked at Adam keenly. "Adam, how's that wound? Excuse me, gentlemen, let me take a moment to check his arm." The others watched as Dr. Dyer pulled aside the sling and questioned Adam. "Really, I'm quite concerned, Adam. You lost an appreciable amount of blood yesterday, and Lucas should keep an eye on you. You have been, haven't you, Dr. Delacroix?"

"Of course, Dr. Dyer," answered Lucas rather defensively. "He spent a restless night, of course, but his color is good this morning, don't you think?"

Adam, the scowl on his face again, said, "That will be quite enough of this, gentlemen. We have more important matters to discuss than my fool arm. Landra, will you excuse us?"

"But, Adam, I really think I should be as informed as possible if I'm to help at the council meeting—"

One of the other men who had followed Lucas and Dr. Dyer into the room stepped forward. He was not a very tall man, but what he lacked in height he made up in girth. The front of his dark coat strained across his broad middle, and he spoke in a pompous tone. "My dear Miss Cole, surely you can understand that we have things to discuss that are not all proper for your tender ears. Rest assured you will be informed of any information we deem necessary for you to be in possession of if we decide it is advantageous for you to be present at the meeting on Tuesday."

Landra stared at the man, whom she had promptly dubbed Dr. Lardbelly. "But—"

"I believe it would be best if you leave us now, Landra," Adam said, not unkindly, but with a definite firmness.

She looked at the men, and it seemed to her that all of them were presenting a solid, masculine front against which she had no defense but retreat—for the moment. Her voice soft, and with a conscious effort to underplay her Yankee accent, she said with an enormous sweet dignity, "Please excuse me, gentlemen, I must see to things in the kitchen. You'll be wanting some refreshment, I'm sure." Landra gave them the full effect of her smile, the brilliant sparkle of those green eyes. For the dazzling moment it took for her to walk proudly to the door, the men saw only a soft, beautiful woman intent on seeing to their comfort and bending to their wishes. They were mercifully unaware of the steel-cored individual who looked out at them from those bewitching eyes; she had a determination any one of them would have been proud to claim. She closed the door softly behind her and heard the immediate buzz of conversation as she leaned against it for a moment.

"Miss Cole—Landra—if you'll come into the kitchen, I'll make you some breakfast." Rose stood uncertainly a short distance away in the dimness of the hallway. Landra followed her, very glad at that moment there was another woman in the house.

CHAPTER 13

Landra glanced around the kitchen, as apprehensive about seeing Jimmy and Anson dePaul as she had been about seeing Adam earlier. Rose must have read her look, for she said, "They're out in the old kitchen. We've had to bandage Jimmy's eyes to keep out the sunlight, and I'll have to go in a little while to start the hot packs again. Anson's watching him; he's grown very fond of Jimmy in the past year. You do, you know, when there's a common bond such as we have—" She stopped, and Landra felt a sudden rush of compassion.

"You've grown very fond of Jimmy, too, haven't you?" she asked Rose softly.

"Fond of him? I love him more than life itself." As she spoke, a change came over her, and she became almost beautiful. Landra forgot the limp softness of the girl's plain brown hair, the wan, colorless complexion. For a moment there were spots of bright color in her cheeks, blooming like the flower she was named for. Her eyes were almost fierce with longing, a deeper blue than they had been before.

"Then why—" Landra hesitated, for what she was thinking was really none of her business. But then she plunged recklessly on, "Why don't you marry? If you both have Hansen's disease, what harm can it do? If only one of you had contracted it, that would be terrible. Then the only thing to do would be to give each other up for the protection of the one who . . ."

As she watched Rose's face, a sudden thought struck her. Perhaps she was taking too much for granted. She had really blundered if Jimmy did not return Rose's love. But since she had already blundered this far, she asked slowly, "Is it Jimmy? Doesn't he—?"

"He loves me, if that's what you're wondering!" answered Rose, her eyes ablaze. "He would have married me long ago; he begged me to before his sight started to go! But now he doesn't even ask anymore. I almost wish I'd done it, married him when we could. But, oh . . . it's all so horrible, and impossible!" She sank into a chair by the table and laid her head on her arms. Her thin shoulders shook violently with sobbing.

Landra stood uncertainly. She wanted very much to help the poor girl, to go to her and put a comforting arm around her shoulders and say something. But she seemed rooted to the spot. An ancient, nameless fear stayed her as surely as if she were chained. She didn't want to touch Rose. The fact reared its ugly head in her mind and leered at her.

It was the same as when she was a child and one of the little boys from town had come to deliver eggs. Landra, who couldn't have been more than five, persuaded him to stay and play. He'd noticed there were many Negro servants at Greenlea, and being from a poor family, naturally his parents had no servants, black or white. As they gathered chinaberries for a war, he had told her something that had been told him often enough; and whether or not he believed it was of little consequence at the time. She could still hear his whispered words: "Don't you know that black rubs off? If they touch you, it'll come off on you, and purty soon you'll be black, too! It just oozes up from their insides, and they got lots of it. *Only it comes off* . . ."

For days afterward she had shrunk from Josie, the Negro woman who had been her adoring nurse from birth. Josie had been puzzled; then in the way of servants who are friends as well, she pried the truth from Landra, who had known better, and yet . . . Landra felt that same reluctance now, only worse. It wasn't the silly childish fear of turning black that made her hesitate, and she wasn't five years old. It was the fear of a terrible disease that had killed her sister and obviously had more far-reaching effects than she had ever dreamed.

A quick, almost wordless prayer winged its way from her heart; Landra knew that within herself she was not capable of the real, nurturing love Rose and the others needed. God rewarded her immediately. Before her eyes Rose changed from a threat, a girl with a hidden, loathsome disease, to a person she did not fear in the least. On the contrary, Landra felt the most extraordinary sense of empathy—extraordinary because she had never experienced what Rose suffered. In a flash of intuitive knowledge, Landra was certain it was was because of Bethany. This girl had been with her sister, had suffered with her.

Rose's sobbing had subsided, but she still made pitiful little sounds that wrung Landra's heart. Slowly Landra moved over and placed a hand on her soft hair.

Rose jerked as if she'd been burned, and looked up at Landra. "Aren't you afraid to touch a leper?" she asked harshly.

Landra's hand trembled, but she did not withdraw it. "Yes, I suppose I am," she answered with costly honesty. "But I want to help. I want to be your friend."

"Friend? Friend to a leper?" Her voice rose and Landra could hear a hint of hysteria.

"Rose, something happened to me last night."

Rose forgot her anger momentarily. "What? Was it someone from the town . . . was it because of us?" Her voice sank now to a pained whisper, and Landra could see that even in her misery Rose was a person who thought first of others.

"No, no, it was nothing like that," she hastened to assure her. "It was something good."

The girl's eyes had a sudden shine of new tears. "Good? Nothing good has happened here for a long time."

"I had just found out about Rob, my sister's child, and I'd realized how very hard it must have been for her—"

"It was," interrupted Rose. "I tried to help all I could, but she was way past my help, or anyone's."

Landra nodded. "I know that now, Rose. When Dr. Freman brought me home last night, I felt as though everything was far beyond me, too. But he shared something that changed it all, and me, too."

Rose started to protest, but somehow the look on Landra's face stopped her; she listened, scarcely breathing, as Landra told of her experience the night before. Rose was quiet for a very long time. "I know about God," she said, her voice small. "But, but . . . oh, it seems wrong to say it, but God just didn't help! I tried to pray, but everything was awful anyway with Anson and your sister and Jimmy's eyes. I just gave up."

It was plain that there was a battle going on in Rose's mind; it was also plain that she was not ready to go further, and Landra knew it. But she also knew that if she held to her newly found faith, if Rose could actually see that difference in Landra's life and actions, there would be another opportunity to talk with her. So instead of pressing the point she said, "Tell me about Jimmy, Rose. It might help if you talk about it. I'd like to know how it all happened, and besides, I might be able to understand more about Bethany, too," she finished, her tone soothing.

It had the desired effect on Rose, for she nodded and wiped her eyes. "Maybe you're right. There hasn't been anybody to talk to in such a long while. Jimmy is too bitter, and Anson has trouble talking at all, except about his book. Dr. Jarrett is kind, but he's busy. And your sister was so . . ."

"Yes?" prompted Landra when the girl hesitated, frowning.

"I'm sorry. There doesn't seem to be any good way to say it."

Landra shrugged. "Just tell me the way it was, Rose."

"She was melancholy, Miss Bethany was. Especially after they—he took the baby away. I used to hear her cry, up in the nursery; that helped me make up my mind. Jimmy was wild when I told him no, but I kept hearing her cry."

Landra herself was very near crying again, so she said hastily, "You were going to tell me about Jimmy, Rose. Why was he wild? What did Bethany have to do with it?" Rose sat slumped in the chair, her hands twisting in her lap. If she had some color in her face, her hair styled, and a pretty dress, she would be attractive, if not beautiful. The girl began to speak, expressing the very thought Landra was entertaining.

"I was pretty then, at least Jimmy said so. The nuns let me pick from the clothes people donated to them, and I always got the best ones first. The nuns spoiled me."

"The nuns?"

"Yes, they brought me up. I was one of those babies you read about in the newspapers—left on the doorstep of the convent." A shadowed smile crossed her face. "I may have been an orphan, but I had twenty-eight mothers. There was a lot of unspent love in their hearts, and they gave it freely to me. It was only when I met Jimmy that I even considered leaving the convent. For a while we—the sisters and I—thought I had a calling, to be one of them. But Jimmy changed all that." There was a sweet expression on her face now, and she paused for a moment, remembering.

"He's a musician, you know. He plays the guitar and sings. The first time I saw him he and two others were playing on the street corner." She saw Landra's polite smile and hastened to add, "Oh, it isn't as though he weren't better than that. He is! They were just between jobs, and besides, people throw a lot of money when they play. He didn't speak to me then, but he smiled. Nobody can smile like my Jimmy. But soon after that, I found the first patch on my leg, and . . . and one of the sisters knew right away. She had served in a mission in the Congo, and saw a lot of people who had it. They took me to a doctor, and he made some tests."

"What kind of tests?" Landra knew her interest bordered on morbid curiosity, but she couldn't help herself.

Rose's fingers went up to her ears and she absently rubbed them. "He scraped the skin on my earlobes."

Landra shuddered. "Wasn't that painful?"

"No," said Rose sadly. "It would have been better if it had been. You see, there are patches of skin that don't feel, and that's one reason poor Anson's hands got so awful. He has no feeling in them and did harm to them without knowing it. My earlobes itched some, but the doctor said they're a favorite hiding place for the hateful germ that causes it. Oh, how I hate it! Look at me, can you tell I'm a leper? *Can you?*"

"No," said Landra faintly.

"You may never be able to, and then again, someday I may look like Anson. Oh, I can't bear it! I just can't bear it!"

Landra said the first thing that came to her mind at the awful distress of the poor girl. "For Jimmy—can you bear it for Jimmy?"

It had the desired effect; the girl calmed somewhat. "It would all be worth it if we could be together, married. But it can never be, never."

The anguish in Rose's voice was so terrible Landra could not help whispering, "But why?" She watched as the girl took a scrap of handkerchief from her apron pocket and dabbed at her eyes. When Rose spoke again her words were soft and low, and Landra could see she was reliving the scene, as she probably had done a hundred times. It was not hard to imagine that she, too, was present; it was as though the three of them sat together.

"Jimmy helped them bury Mrs. Jarrett. Afterward he came back here, and sat right there in the chair beside you. I could tell he was shaken something awful. She was a good, gentle lady and we all loved her. I remember what Jimmy said . . ." Rose's eyes seemed to glaze as the memory of that day crept into her mind. She stared at the open window, unseeing. Then she began, slowly relating every detail of the painful memory etched so deeply in her mind.

" 'Rosie,' he said to me, 'It was almost more than a fella can stand, to see Dr. Jarrett like he was. I waited an hour, but he wouldn't leave her grave. He just stood there looking down. Once, when I tried to get him to come in, he looked me in the eye and said it was his fault. "It's my fault she's in there," he said. There wasn't anything I could say to help, Rose.'

"He looked so miserable I got up and went around the table and put my arms around him. He buried his face in me, and he kind of groaned. I wanted to help him so bad. 'Oh, Jimmy, I know how you feel. Dr. Jarrett has done a lot for us. If it wasn't for him, we wouldn't be here at Greenlea, together.' His hair was so soft. I remember how it felt, how I loved the way it curled flat against his neck.

" 'Rose—' He stopped, then drew his head away and stared up into my face. He had the biggest, brownest eyes. I couldn't have looked away if I'd wanted to. 'Rose, I love you so much. Please, let's don't wait anymore . . . let's get married, right away. I'll become a Catholic, like you want, anything! Only let's don't waste any more time. Let's marry, now. Please, Rosie, say you will.' I closed my eyes as he stood up and pulled me close and I felt his lips moving over my face, my mouth. 'Oh, Rose . . . please, I want to love you, I want you to be my wife. . . .'

"I loved him, but when he began to touch me I couldn't stand it. I wanted him to, but I couldn't let him. 'Jimmy, no!'

" 'Why not, love?' he whispered, embracing me again . . . and again. 'Rose, it would be wonderful for you and me. Don't you see, we can at least have each other. There's no need to deny ourselves that. There's no reason.'

"When he tried to kiss me again I pulled away. It was like I had a fever. I couldn't stop shaking. 'Jimmy, don't you see, we can't!'

" 'No, Rose, I don't see. You love me, don't you?'

" 'Yes, of course, but—'

" 'And I love you. Don't do this to us. We don't have anybody or anything but each other.'

" 'Jimmy, if we were to be married, and you were to . . . to love me like you have been, the way I want you to, I—"

" 'That I would, Rose. I'd love you until you forgot this devilish blight that's on us. I'd love you until—'

"I stopped him, and pushed him away from me. 'No, Jimmy. I don't know much about it, and I shouldn't say so, but it would be the joy of my life to let you love me—like that. But we can never be man and wife. There might be children, and I couldn't go through what she did.'

" 'You mean Mrs. Jarrett.'

" 'Yes, Jimmy, I do. You weren't here when they took her baby away; I was. She was like a madwoman. For days on end she cried, and there was nothing I could do for her, nothing anybody could do. She wouldn't eat, and she turned on Dr. Jarrett for a while. She screamed at him and told him she hated him. It was awful! Before . . . she was the gentlest, most lovely lady I ever knew. And afterward, she was so sorry, and desperate to make it up to him. Sometimes even now I think I hear her crying, crying.

" 'I'm not as strong as Mrs. Jarrett. I couldn't decide to have a child and have it snatched away . . . never even to give it nourishment from my horrible, sick body. . . .' How hopeless it all was! I couldn't help it, I couldn't keep the tears from coming.

" 'Don't, Rose, don't! There are ways; we don't have to have babies—' He came close, his arms out, reaching for me.

" 'No! If you come any nearer, if you hold me again, I won't be able to finish.' I put out a hand to keep him away, but he took it and held it tight. 'I—the church won't allow what you speak of, and there is every reason to believe that if we were to marry, there would be children.'

" 'But your church can't want, or believe it's right to bring babies into the world to become . . . lepers?'

" 'I can't question the church, Jimmy, I can't.'

" 'But it's not fair! We're denied the privileges of the poorest, commonest people because we're lepers; do you mean to say we can't even be together?'

"I had to turn my head away. I couldn't stand the pain in his eyes. 'I can't marry you and . . . and arrange not to have babies. It's against everything the sisters taught me, against my very faith. God will help us.'

" 'God!' he said, his voice hoarse and awful. 'God? How can there be a God when—'

" 'Hush, Jimmy, don't talk like that! I'll help you, I'll still love you forever. We—'

"But he wasn't listening. He let go of my hand, and without looking at me again, left the room."

Rose sat very still, her hands clasped tightly on the smooth golden surface of the oak table top. "He left, Landra, and didn't come back to Greenlea for weeks. Oh, I imagined all kinds of things, that he might have done like Mrs. Jarrett, and given up— Oh, I'm sorry, please forgive me!"

"It's all right, Rose. Jimmy didn't give up, did he? He came back."

"Yes, he came back. But he never again mentioned marriage to me. It wasn't long after that he began having the pain in his eyes, and Dr. Jarrett told us what the final stage would be— blindness. So now, all I can do is care for him like a nurse. He accepts it, but he never says he loves me; how I wish he would say it again!"

"Perhaps his silence is the only way he is able to bear the situation, Rose. He surely still loves you. Love doesn't die that easily." Landra rose suddenly, feeling stifled in the high-ceilinged room. There were windows, but they were high and small, and she felt the need to be out-of-doors.

"I think I'll go for a walk, maybe where my sister is buried. Rose, where is her grave?"

Rose nodded. "It's in the corner of the big meadow, by the double oaks. You know the spot?"

Flooded with memories, Landra could only nod.

CHAPTER 14

The afternoon sun was warm, but a gentle breeze lifted the loose tendrils of hair about her neck as she walked toward the back meadow. The May sunshine warmed her back and she trailed slowly through the soft pink and yellow buttercups, past the morning glory vines, their blue blossoms now closed after a brief awakening during the cooler morning hours.

A brilliant green carpet of clover spread at her feet as she drew closer to the twin oaks, and she breathed deeply the sweet smell of the crushed mauve flowers where she walked. The only sound was the drone of bees, intent on raiding the limitless supply of nectar all around. Honeysuckle, its creamy flowers abundant, covered the fence that bordered the meadow. From the beginning four generations ago, there had been a meadow, a lea. It was from this meadow that the house had gotten its name, Greenlea.

How she and Bethany had loved it here, far from Josie's watchful eyes! The inummerable scoldings for the emerald stains on pristine white frocks were never enough to deter them from spending many hours here—Landra making endless chains with the fragrant clover blossoms, Bethany sitting primly with her back to one of the old oaks, dreaming girlish dreams about when she would marry and be the mistress of Greenlea. Yes, Bethany had loved it here.

Landra saw it then, the simple, gracefully carved stone with these words on it: Bethany Cole Jarrett, Beloved Wife, 1870–1900. She placed her hand on the cool, smooth stone, thinking that Bethany would dream forever now beneath the gnarled old oak trees, forever shaded by their spreading branches. Landra could not have said how long she stood there, but so deep was she in thoughts and memories, she was startled to hear a man's voice, very near, say, "I've been watching you." It was Hollis.

"Oh, I didn't see you—"

"I know." He came closer, a concerned look on his face as he glanced at the inscription on the headstone, then at her pale, sad countenance. "You loved your sister a great deal."

"Everyone loved Bethany. It was impossible not to."

"Even when you tried not to?"

She looked up at him, frowning. "What do you mean by that?"

"Nothing, nothing," he said quickly. "Forgive me. I was only thinking of my own circumstances; my older brother always excelled in everything, was an abominably good sport on every occasion, was even nice to me. I did my level best to hate him with absolutely no success whatever," he finished cheerfully.

Landra smiled. "Maybe you do understand, after all."

"Maybe a little," he agreed. He looked thoughtful, then said, "The hardest thing must have been giving up the baby. He's a beautiful child. Landra, I—" His hands were in his pockets, then out again, then jammed in. "Well, I didn't say anything yesterday; you seemed to have so much to take in as it was. But I'm glad it was your sister's baby, and not Carrie Chaumont's, and I'm glad Dr. Jarrett wasn't guilty of—"

"So am I," Landra broke in softly. "So am I. I only wish I hadn't even suspected it of him." Her hand still gripped the cool marble surface of the stone.

"Are you coming to terms with it, Landra? Can I help?"

She took a deep breath and met his eyes. "I'm just beginning to. Somehow after last night I thought it would be easier, but . . . but it still hurts terribly."

He put his hand comfortingly on her shoulder. "Of course it does."

"And this has been a difficult morning. Poor Adam. He tried so hard to answer questions about what killed Beth and I'm not sure I can face the answers, by the way. It's horrible, *indescribable*, what they have to go through."

Soberly he nodded. "I've been asking some questions of my own, and you're right, the answers are pretty awful."

Landra stared past him, her eyes not seeing the lush green lea, the fresh blue sky. "Then I listened as Rose told me the most heartbreaking story you can imagine, and there was absolutely nothing I could do."

His fingers touched her cheek, lining her jaw, until they were beneath her chin and he lifted her face. "Nothing?"

Her eyes met his. "That's not true." She smiled again, now, a tremulous smile to be sure, but real nonetheless. "I did tell her what happened to me last night."

"Good, good! And?"

"She wasn't ready to let God work in her heart yet, but she knows, now, that I care, and I'll be able to talk to her again, I'm sure of it. All I have to do is be open to the opportunity, as—" She broke off, then said, a little breathless at the look on his face, "As you were last night."

He was very close, and she could see the sun glinting on the unruly lock of hair that dangled on his broad forehead. His gaze was intent, as though he didn't remember her face, and was trying to fix it in his mind now. When she said as much, he shook his head slowly. "Not at all. I'll never forget your face. It's just that I could never get enough of looking at it, either. Those long lashes, the green of your eyes—how can they be that color?" He laughed wonderingly and she started to say something but he rushed on. "And last but absolutely not least, your mouth. Surely you don't rouge your lips?" At the quick shake of her head he said, "I thought not. . . ."

He bent down and touched her lips with his, then drew back, a smile making a small dimple appear momentarily just to the left of his mouth. "Landra, you may not be ready to hear this, but do you remember when I said I loved you last night?"

"Yes . . ."

"You assumed I meant it in another way, and I do. But I also find that since Denis Chaumont brought you to my house, so pale and shaken, your courage obvious even in a very frightening situation, I've not had you out of my mind. All day long, I try to pretend I'm a doctor and useful; when I go to bed at night and dream, it's always of you. And when I wake up, the first thing I think of is you. I love you, Landra."

His kiss was different this time; it began as slowly, as tenderly, but deepened, and Landra found she could not help but respond. Sheltered and protected as a girl, shut away with an invalid mother as a young woman, she had never felt the tumult of emotion that ran through her now. As he drew away slightly, his eyes smiling down into hers, she murmured, "I . . . I think I love you, too!"

"You only think?" He laughed outright. "I'll just have to persuade you." He kissed her again and again, as if to convince her. "I'm going to fall down if we don't sit down," he finally said, laughing.

Landra put a trembling hand to her face. "I feel a bit faint myself."

He took her hand in his, and with his free one he smoothed her brow with long, gentle fingers. "I must prescribe a remedy."

"And what is that?" Landra asked softly, giddy with happiness.

"Just sit down here in the grass. . . . Then think of how much I love you."

She followed his suggestion, then chuckled. "I don't think this is going to work! Either the sun or my thoughts is making me more dizzy than ever."

"Me, too," he admitted, leaning on one elbow to look into her face. She gazed into his face. "Landra, if my father were here—and I'm glad he's not!—he would say, 'Now, Hollis, you musn't go off half-cocked.' I know it has been an indecently short time since we met. But there's something I believe you should know."

"Tell me, Hollis."

"I asked God to lead me to a woman who would be willing to share my life, one whose life I could share as well. I sort of had in mind a nice-looking girl with a nice background and a nice family who would think I was a nice young man . . ."

Landra laughed with him. "And what you got is a headstrong redhead with no family at all, and who isn't the least bit nice!"

"Ah, that's not so at all. You are exactly what I wanted; I just didn't have enough faith to ask Him for a . . . a wonderful girl like you, who's warm, and caring—and beautiful." He quickly kissed her again, then pulled her to her feet. "We'd better get you back to the house or I just might—"

"You might what?"

He stood looking down at her, a mischievous grin on his face, in his eyes. "Oh, go into Noirville and check at the livery stable . . . for a white horse so I can come back here and carry you off!"

"You wouldn't!" His arms circled her loosely; she stood within their safety with profound gratitude.

"No, as a matter of fact, I wouldn't. When I told you that

evening at my house that you were safe with me, I meant it with all my heart, and I do now. I want to take care of you, be with you. Landra, will you—"

Breathlessly she waited for him to go on, and when he didn't she saw that he was staring beyond her shoulder. It was then that she saw Adam and Lucas Delacroix striding purposefully toward them.

Lucas spoke first. "I thought I warned you, Freman. Are you going to leave now, or do we have to—" He broke off and took another step toward Hollis, fists clenched.

"Don't!" said Landra. "He only came to see me—is that so terrible?"

"I doubt that's his real reason for coming," said Adam, his expression grim.

Landra stared at him, hurt. "Do you mean to say it's inconceivable that a young man would want to call on me, that he would have an ulterior motive?"

"Well, I—"

Landra interrupted Adam angrily. "No matter what you think, Dr. Freman came because he wanted to see me. Isn't that true, Hollis?" She looked up at him, realizing suddenly that one arm was still protectively tight around her shoulders.

"It most definitely is," he responded immediately.

"Well, whether you're here to court, or spy, or both, doesn't matter. You'd better leave at once. I warned you last night!" said Lucas.

"I think he's right," said Adam. "This is really not the proper time for you to be making social calls, Dr. Freman. And as to any other purpose you may have had in coming, I'll tell you frankly, we'll do our best to see that you get nothing that would help our opposition at the council meeting. You do understand, don't you?"

"Yes, *I* do. But, Dr. Jarrett, I'm afraid *you* don't. If you'd just give me a chance to explain—"

"Have they approached you, asking you to testify for them?"

Lucas' blunt question caught Hollis off guard. "Yes, they have but it's not—"

"Young man," said Adam with a menace in his voice that Landra had never heard before, "you'd better get off this property, and fast, or I'll not be responsible for the consequences."

"But, sir—"

Landra, sensing that Adam and Lucas were close to physical

violence, said urgently, "Please, Hollis, I think it would be better if you left now. Please?"

"All right, Landra. But I won't be far away." He pulled her close for just an instant, then strode away.

"If he knows what's good for him, he *will* make it far away," muttered Lucas as they watched Hollis go to the horse he had tethered to a nearby tree, swing up, and gallop away. The two men looked significantly at each other and began to walk back toward the house, speaking in low tones. Landra followed, unable to hear anything but snatches.

"—he's bright, there's no telling what they've offered him to—"

"There's got to be a way to counteract his testimony . . ." This from Adam.

They were very near the house when she saw old Sam'l hobbling up, nodding and smiling broadly at Adam, who said, "Sam'l, how are you?"

"Fine, suh, jes' fine. I cum out to see if you needed any hep. I done heard 'bout the shooting!" A puzzled frown on his wrinkled old face, he looked at Adam's bandaged arm. "I didn't hardly believe whut folks told me."

"It's true, all right," answered Adam grimly.

"Come into the kitchen, Sam'l, and Rose will get you something to drink," said Landra, trying to sort out the multitude of emotions assailing her, wishing she knew more about Adam's accusing remarks concerning Hollis.

"Oh, no, ma'am; I'll jes' set out chere on the back porch a spell afore I goes on."

All four of them walked to the back of the house, and watched as Sam'l settled his thin old body on the edge of the porch, legs dangling. They were about to go in when suddenly he sniffed loudly and said, "I smells sumpin'."

Lucas rolled his eyes and said, "I'm going to the lab. I've had quite enough social contact for today," he finished, not bothering to hide his sarcasm as he went inside, slamming the door behind him.

But Adam asked kindly, "Is it something good, or something bad, Sam'l?"

"Sumpin' bad, mighty bad. Don't you git a whiff, now and then?"

The air was warm and there was the heavy scent of flowers in it. But underneath, brief and intermittent, there was an ugly hint of something else. Landra caught it, and her lips curled in distaste.

"What is it?" she asked. "It smells like . . . something dead."

"You mighty right," said Sam'l. "That whut it is."

Adam didn't speak as he watched Sam'l heave himself painfully to his feet and hobble down the steps. The porch was perhaps three feet off the ground, and the space below was covered with a peeling, white-painted wooden lattice screen. There was an opening on the left side of the steps, and Sam'l undid the latch and crawled through on his hands and knees.

"Adam, do you know what he's doing?" asked Landra anxiously.

"I'm afraid so."

"What?"

"You'll see in a moment if you've got the nerve to stay. If you don't have a strong stomach, I'd suggest you leave right now, before he—"

But Sam'l was already emerging, a shiny object in his hand. Adam went over to help the old man out.

Landra stared at the thing in Sam'l's hand. He shook his head in anger. "Gris gris! Bad, this is very bad gris gris."

"Adam . . ." Landra felt her stomach lurch.

Sam'l looked at her pityingly. "You never seen nothin' like this here?" When she shook her head he went on, his crackly old voice almost chanting the words. "You take a dead black cat, take off all the hair and wrop it up in silver paper . . . stuff the mouf with melted red wax; make magic words over it, then put it under somebody's house. It's a spell."

Landra shook her head in disbelief. "A magic spell? Whatever for?"

Adam, his voice devoid of expression, explained. "This particular gris gris is to make whoever lives in the house move. It's supposed to be quite effective."

"But that's ridiculous, superstitious nonsense!" Landra burst out. She watched as the old man, holding his disturbing burden gingerly, walked over to the overgrown garden and buried it there. When he came back, he stood hesitantly before them.

Adam said, "What is it, Sam'l? Is there something else on your mind?"

Sam'l took several deep breaths. Sighing heavily, he said, "They done run me out'n my house. I jes' cum to say so long."

"That's terrible! Why would they do such a thing, unless

. . ." Landra trailed off, realizing that the reason was almost certainly because Sam'l had been a servant at Greenlea so long, and the angry mood extended to everyone connected to it or Elkhorn. She glanced at Adam, whose mouth was hard and set.

"Where are you headed?" he asked.

Sam'l looked at Adam for a long time, then answered, "Guess I'll go on to my sister's over to Bogalusa."

"But, Adam," Landra protested. "We can't just let him go, he's too—"

"Too old?" Sam'l supplied. "Yes'm, I shore is, but there ain't no place for me to stay. They smashed up my little house. I'll just mosey on."

Landra said firmly, "You'll do no such thing. There's room for you here, isn't there, Adam?"

Adam shrugged his shoulders and said quietly aside to her, "Of course, but he'll never stay here. He's as afraid of contracting the disease as anyone alive." He opened the door and started in.

"But you can't just let him go; he's an old man, and he's been faithful. We've got to do something!"

He stared hard at her. There was a passionate determination in her words that was intensified by the brilliance of her eyes, the upward tilt of her chin. "I admire your desire to help him, but nothing on earth could induce that old man to stay here at Greenlea. Don't you realize that added to his fear of the disease is the fact that he really believes in the stupid curse? He would never have touched it if he hadn't believed that it would be more dangerous for me, as the head of the house, to do so." His voice softened a little. "He's transferred that deep loyalty he felt for your family and Bethany to me, obviously. I'll go and get some money. He'll need it."

"Money! What he needs is . . . is a friend!"

He didn't answer but went inside, leaving her alone with the old man, who had stood abjectly as they were talking.

Not ten minutes later, Adam, his mind already on other problems, came down the hall from the lab, money in hand. There he met Landra, followed by Sam'l.

She was saying earnestly, "I know you'll be comfortable in that little room on this side of the kitchen, Sam'l. All right?"

Sam'l nodded wordlessly, his eyes large in the black, seamed face. He stopped at the sight of Adam, who frowned in disbelief, then said slowly, "I never would have believed it. How did you persuade him to stay?"

"I just explained how I felt about the situation, and that I'm staying. Anyway, you may need all the help you can get. You may even be grateful for the support of an old man and a weak, helpless woman before this thing is over."

She took Sam'l's arm gently and they went past Adam, whose face bore a speculative expression. Landra looked at that moment like anything but a weak, helpless woman; even Adam could see that.

CHAPTER 15

Landra was awake almost instantly. The knock and whispered voices from down the hall were muted, but enough to rouse her from sleep. Her mother had always said a cat walking could waken Landra. She stared into the darkness, straining to hear, to decide who was speaking. Adam's deep voice was recognizable; the other must be Rose.

She got up and put her wrapper on, drawing it about her as if she were cold. The room still held the muggy heat of the day, and as she eased the door open a light, cool breeze wafted up from somewhere below.

"Adam?" she called out as she saw him at the head of the stairs, closely followed by Rose. "Is something wrong?"

Rose held a kerosene lamp in her hand, and by its soft light Landra could see the drawn expression on Adam's face. He halted momentarily, and although he seemed to be looking at Landra, he did not really see her as he spoke. "It's Anson. He's bad."

Before Landra could answer, he had hurried down and she was left alone. She withdrew into her room and stood indecisively for a moment, then quickly dressed and went out into the dark hallway. She had brought no lamp or candle, and the long, wide staircase was completely shadowed. It was cooler here than in her room, yet her anxiety at the memory of Adam's expression, combined with the darkness, almost suffocated her.

When she reached the lab she remembered that thought, for even with the door closed she could hear the horrible rasping sounds of someone who *was* suffocating. She opened the door and was shocked at the sight of Anson dePaul lying on the long table.

141

The anguished, labored sound of Anson's struggle to draw air into his lungs filled the lamp-lit room. Landra could see the extreme pallor of the man's ruined face beneath the hideous welts, as well as the bluish tinge which signified the lack of oxygen in his blood. That he could breathe at all was amazing, for the bridge of his nose had long since fallen in. She caught a glimpse of the fear in his eyes—fear of death, or of life, she could not tell.

"Adam! What's happening?" she cried.

"He's choking to death," was the grim answer. He turned to Rose, who still held the lamp with a fierce grip. "Rose, where's Lucas? Didn't you waken him? You know I can't—" He glanced at his wounded arm, a helpless, angry expression on his face. "If we don't get some air into his lungs *now*, it will be too late! Where's Lucas?" he repeated.

Rose had turned white. "He's . . . he's not here," she whispered. "I looked in his room, but he's not here!"

The gravity of the situation hit Adam first, but the two women were not long in realizing that the man on the table was as good as dead if something was not done immediately.

Adam spoke then. "Rose, you'll have to help me." He looked down at his right hand, flexed it a couple of times, and winced as he was unable to even close his fist. "I'll tell you exactly what to do . . . it's very simple, really."

But Rose was staring first at the man on the table and then at Adam, with an open-mouthed look of horror. "I couldn't, I couldn't! I can't stand blood . . ." She stood for a long moment, her slight body shaking with the dread of what he had suggested, then fled from the room. "I have to see to Jimmy. Jimmy might need me—" Her frightened words echoed down the hall in her wake.

Landra watched in stunned silence as Adam began hurriedly, clumsily, with his left hand, to gather up a shining scalpel, a bottle of disinfectant, and a long silver tube which was cut at a slant on the end. He had asked Rose, but Rose was gone; she had fled in dazed fear. There was no one left but Adam, and her. Landra tried to push away the thought that Adam might ask her to . . . no, it was not possible. She couldn't, any more than Rose could.

As he worked he talked. "To purposefully cut a man's throat sounds pretty bad, I'll admit, but tracheotomies have been done successfully countless times, even in emergency situations. Of course, it would be infinitely better in a hospital, under aseptic conditions. But even if we could get him to a hospital in time, they wouldn't allow Anson to contaminate their hallowed walls," he said bitterly. "This," he held up the silver tube, "is a tracheotomy tube, a cannula, and will serve as his windpipe, or trachea, until he can breathe normally on his own again. It must be inserted below the obstruction that is causing the trouble."

Landra was listening carefully; vaguely she perceived that Adam was speaking for her benefit, subconsciously aware that he was not able to perform the surgery he was preparing for. She felt almost paralyzed with tension at the awesome implications.

He moved the lamps as near to Anson as possible, speaking softly to the suffering man, telling him to relax, that it wouldn't be long. The strong, blunt fingers of his left hand were swabbing Anson's throat with antiseptic soaked cotton, and he spoke sharply to Landra. "What are you waiting for? Surely you realize it's imperative to be as clean as possible. Wash your hands—scrub them—and hurry."

Even as she moved to the basin, poured water into it and scrubbed at her hands with the yellow, ugly-smelling bar of soap, Landra kept telling herself it was all a terrible dream, brought on by the past days' experiences, that she would waken and find it was all a dream.

But it was no dream. Landra dried her hands on a towel and stood waiting as Adam took the scalpel in his right hand. She held her breath, for she saw that he was going to try, at least. Slowly, painfully, he closed his fingers around the slender handle, his jaw set with the effort. Small beads of perspiration broke out on his forehead, but he stepped close to the table and placed the knife on Anson's throat. Then his hand began to tremble and he grasped it with his left, but it was no use. The scalpel clattered to the floor and he stared at it in anguish.

Anson began to gasp even harder, and Adam stepped quickly over to the small cabinet that held his surgical instruments and drew out another scalpel identical to the one on the floor. He began to speak quite calmly to Landra. "There's no reason whatever why you can't make the initial incision. I'll help you with the bleeding—we'll have to make sure it isn't allowed to seep into the opening in the trachea and into his lungs. Here," he said, and handed her the knife.

It was very smooth, and quite cool. She stared at it for an endless second; it was impossible that he should expect her to . . . but he did. "Hurry, Landra, please hurry!"

"What . . . what do I have to do?" She did not look at Anson's face, she made herself deaf to the now even more ugly, rasping sound of his breathing. She allowed Adam to place the scalpel properly into her nerveless hand, and then felt a small, comforting second of warmth as he clasped his own around it.

His voice was deep and sure as he gave careful, precise instructions. "You must insert the knife into the neck over the trachea in the midline, no higher." He took hold of Anson's chin and pulled it gently up, exposing his throat. Surprisingly enough, the disease had not blemished the skin there, and as long as Landra kept her eyes on the area between the man's chin and where his collar was open, she could make herself forget what was above, forget the pitiful, claw-like hands clutching the side of the table in an agony near to death itself.

Adam's quiet voice continued. "The incision must be made in the midline from a point below the Adam's apple downward." He placed a finger on Anson's throat, indicating the exact point at which she must begin. Begin? Plunge the knife into the man's throat, to kill him with the cure? She felt a terrible, irresistible urge to laugh; it bubbled unbidden to her lips.

"Stop that!" commanded Adam harshly. "It's been done before and you can do it now, if you don't lose control."

The shock of his words cleared Landra's brain suddenly, and made her aware of two things. She knew she could not do as he said no matter what he thought, and knew that Hollis Freman was surely outside, not far away. Hadn't he said he would be? "I'll be right back," she said breathlessly.

"Landra—" said Adam, the desperation making his voice even harsher.

But she was already out of the laboratory, her feet flying down the hall and out the kitchen door into the night. "Hollis? Hollis!" she called out. "Are you there? Please . . ."

In the darkness of midnight the stillness was a living, breathing thing; she felt a sob rise in her throat. Was it possible she was wrong, that he was not still keeping watch? Another endless moment, then she heard steps, and his voice saying, "I'm coming, Landra."

Even though she wanted to collapse into his arms and sob, she pulled at him instead, almost dragging him into the house.

"It's Anson, the man Adam has been treating; he needs a tracheotomy, and Adam can't do it because his injured arm is—" She was quite suddenly out of breath.

"I understand." As he followed her down the dark hallway he said, "Will he . . . I mean do you think he'll allow me to help? He did order me off the property, and I obviously disregarded those orders."

"I hoped you would! Oh, Hollis, he wanted *me* to perform the operation, and I . . . I thought of you. Hurry, please!"

They burst into the room and Hollis said tersely, "Landra has told me some of the situation, Dr. Jarrett, and even though I've not done the procedure before, if you'll talk me through it, I'm sure that together we can manage." With one fluid, graceful movement he tore off his coat, washed his hands and took the scalpel that was in Adam's useless hand.

Adam said nothing whatever about his earlier animosity, just gave instructions to Hollis in a precise, low voice that showed the strain he was under. Landra shrank back, a sick little feeling assailing her as she saw him boldly, quickly press the knife into Anson's throat exactly as Adam directed. But she was unable to close her eyes at the sight of the instant welling of blood that came from the incision.

Landra stared in horrified fascination as Adam handed the necessary instruments to Hollis; she could do nothing but lean weakly against the rough, whitewashed wall as the two men battled time and death. Anson's response was immediate and gratifying. There was a whooshing, sucking sound as the air bypassed the upper obstruction and was drawn into the lungs; then as Hollis inserted the tube into the wound, the sound of great deep breaths gratefully taken.

"There," said Adam. "No doubt the nodules have swollen his laryngeal passage to such an extent that he was unable to get enough air to sustain himself." He watched as Hollis fastened the tube securely with a white tape that encircled the man's neck. "We can only hope he is due for a remission of the symptoms very soon, and the swelling will subside. If not . . ."

"Sir, has he had this severe a complication before?" Hollis asked.

Adam nodded gravely. "Not of this exact nature, of course, but several times Anson has been on the brink of death. He's a strong-minded man." Absorbed in Anson's life-threatening situation, Adam seemed to have forgotten the angry words that had passed between him and Hollis that afternoon.

As Hollis washed his hands he said, a frown on his face, "It's barbaric that you must treat him here. He should be in a hospital, with aseptic conditions, and nurses, and—"

"Exactly." Adam fixed his black eyes on Hollis. "Those who are opposing the establishing of the hospital at Elkhorn don't seem to recognize that very real fact, Dr. Freman." Landra could see that Adam was now recalling the earlier discussion, and realized he had been working with someone who was not in sympathy with the thing he had given his life fully to. "And you, Dr. Freman, what exactly have you decided about our hospital? Do you feel we are the scourge of the community, as your esteemed colleagues do? I'm not going to deny I'm grateful for your help tonight, but I will not back down an inch in my conviction that without a hospital, some of these people are doomed."

Hollis looked around him at the orderly, but obviously inadequate room; his eyes came to rest on the man who lay on the table before him. Anson dePaul's skin was no longer tinged with blue; the life-giving air whistled with comforting regularity into the silver tube in his neck. Disaster had been averted by the merest chance; though he was shocked by the terrible ruin of the stricken man's face, as a doctor he was more appalled by the primitive conditions for an operation of such a serious nature. There was a look of almost total exhaustion in Adam's eyes as Hollis turned finally to him. "Dr. Jarrett, please sit down. You look ready to fall down." He moved to the older man, took his arm, and led him to a chair. "He'll be all right at least for a while, won't he?"

Adam slumped into the chair. "I appreciate your helping Anson," he said, his good hand holding the injured arm close to his body. "But if you don't mind my asking, why did you do it?"

"For the same reason you would: I'm a doctor. Not a good one yet, but I will be. The man needed me," he finished simply.

"That's certainly true. But what about your feelings—yours and the others?"

Hollis went to stand by Landra and put a supporting arm around her; she leaned into his gratefully. "I think you have misjudged me, Dr. Jarrett," he answered. "I am not, and never have been, a part of this *opposition,* as you call them."

"But I heard that you have been approached, that they offered you money as well as a substantial number of referral patients if you would cooperate," countered Adam, his black eyes boring into Hollis.

Hollis met his eyes squarely. "You're right on that count. They did made such an offer. But," he hastened to add at the expression on Adam's face, "this time I will finish what you didn't allow me to this afternoon. All right?" Adam nodded. "I told them," Hollis continued, "that I didn't know enough about the situation to make a decision, that I would have to find out just what you proposed to do, and then make up my own mind. After tonight, I won't have much trouble doing that."

Landra looked up at him. "What do you mean?"

"That should be obvious. The need for a facility to help men and women like Anson should be a priority. I, for one, would be proud if you'd let me help, Dr. Jarrett."

"I believe you mean that," murmured Adam.

"I do. I don't know exactly what is involved, but no doubt you'll tell me." His grasp on Landra's shoulder tightened. "There's something else."

"Yes?" Adam's gaze on him was different now; the hostility was gone and there was a thoughtful, assessing look in his eyes. "Go on, man, what is it?"

"Sir, at the risk of being precipitous . . ." He halted, and Landra noticed with a quick surge of endearing feeling that his ears had reddened. But he straightened manfully and said, "I tend to get a little pompous at times, or so my mother says. Dr. Jarrett, I feel that although Landra and I have known each other for only a short time, it's long enough to know I care deeply for her. Her mother and father—and her sister—are not here to give their blessing, so . . . well, I would like your permission to pay court to Landra," he finished in a rush.

Gravely Adam surveyed him, then Landra. "Is this what you want, Landra?"

"I—" Landra began; then, as she looked up into Hollis' face, said, "Yes, it is, Adam."

"Then I give you leave." Adam stood and swayed a little on his feet.

"You really should be resting, sir," said Hollis. "I think perhaps—" He was interrupted as Lucas burst into the room.

"How is Anson? Were you able to get the procedure done in time? What is *he* doing here?" he asked, seeing Hollis nearby. Even as he spoke Lucas was moving to where Anson lay. The sound of the desperately ill man's deep, now rhythmic breathing was the only audible thing in the room for a space of time. Lucas' fingers were on his pulse and he watched him intently. "We can only hope for a remission. His pulse is strong."

Landra remembered that Adam had said the same thing. "What do you mean, Lucas, when you say *remission*? He's really likely to get better?"

But Lucas answered seriously, "Why, yes, of course he could get better. And sometimes, even after terrible damage such as Anson has suffered, there is a spontaneous disappearance of all acute symptoms, leaving what is very like an immunity for a while. Have you never heard of a burnt-out case?" At Landra's slow shake of her head in denial, he said, "You must admit the title is appropriate. There are times when Hansen's bacillus seems to lose its violence; it's as though, having wreaked almost total havoc with its victim, it subsides, leaving . . ." He glanced at Anson then at Adam, and evidently decided against saying anything further. "Good lord, Adam, you're not in very good shape yourself. Is the arm giving you much pain?" He stepped over to where Adam leaned against the wall and replaced the injured arm in the empty sling.

"Lucas," began Landra, then, finding she didn't know exactly how to phrase the question in her mind, she hesitated. He turned toward her expectantly, his eyes flicking over Hollis. She finally said, "You didn't tell me the wound in his arm affected his hand. Is it . . . is it permanent?"

The two men glanced at each other; then Lucas answered. "We hope not, of course. There is certain nerve involvement, but sometimes these things heal themselves and there are no noticeable aftereffects."

Adam shrugged. "It would be no great loss to the medical profession if it were true. I'm a research scientist, not a surgeon."

"But it—"

Lucas interrupted Landra and turned a hostile expression toward Hollis. "What I'd like to know is why you're here, Freman. I thought we made it perfectly clear this afternoon that you were not to come onto the premises again."

Hollis' chin lifted, but he didn't reply. It was Adam who answered for him. "It seems we've misjudged Dr. Freman, Lucas. He hasn't sold out to the opposition after all."

"How can we be certain?" Lucas' hard question was shot at Hollis.

"Who do you think performed the operation on Anson, Lucas?" asked Adam wearily. "He has stated unequivocally that he wants to join us. I can't think what would have happened if he hadn't been 'on the premises,' as you put it."

Lucas had the good grace to flush. "I should have been here."

"But you weren't." Quite suddenly Adam's face sagged, and it was all too apparent he was close to total exhaustion.

"Go upstairs, Adam, and get some rest," ordered Lucas. "I'll see to things here."

"But the cannula—"

"I'll change the inner tube as often as it needs to be done. I'm perfectly capable of tending Anson," he said, an edge to his tone.

Just as firmly Hollis added, "And I'm here to help." His blue eyes were not cold, but the warmth Landra had reveled in was gone, replaced by a look of steely determination.

The two men eyed each other; then Lucas looked away first. "Fine. We need help, God knows. Go upstairs, Adam," he repeated. "I . . . we'll see to Anson."

Adam nodded and as he made his way to the door, stumbled. It was Hollis who said, "I'll go with you. Be back in a moment, Landra."

But he had to wait as Adam retraced his faltering steps to Anson's side and laid a gentle hand on his shoulder. "Sleep if you can, Anson, you need to sleep."

There was a barely perceptible nod from the man, more in gratitude for Adam's touch than in agreement that sleep was possible. He was alive . . . he was still alive, and totally unable to decide if he was glad or not. Somehow he sensed Adam was aware of his feelings, and it helped—a little.

They watched Adam and Hollis leave, then after a brief hesitation Landra said, "I'll be glad to spell you if you need me, Lucas." She was still feeling the shock of her inadequacy, of being totally helpless in the face of Anson's need.

Lucas turned and regarded her steadily for a moment. "You mean that, don't you?"

"Yes, I do. I want very badly to help, just as Hollis does." She tucked a straggling lock of hair behind her ear, realizing she was very anxious for him to accept her help; his acceptance was somehow vital to her.

Before he could frame a reply Rose came into the room, cast a fearful glance at Anson, and said breathlessly, "Dr. Delacroix, is he . . . did the operation go all right?"

"Yes, Rose, Anson is holding his own." His tone was noticeably softer, kinder than when he spoke to either Landra or Hollis. "Did you need something?"

"I don't want to take you away if Anson needs you, but Jimmy is having a lot of pain. I've been applying the hot packs, but it's getting worse. Oh, I don't know how I can stand it, and it's not even me that's hurting!"

Her anguish was palpable in the quiet room. Lucas turned to Landra. "Will you be able to sit with Anson? If not, I can wait until Dr. Freman comes down."

"No, I can do it. You go on to Jimmy." Landra moved to Anson's side and stood resolutely by the table. "I'll call you if there's the slightest change in his breathing."

For a moment he seemed to be caught between loyalties, then he nodded and left with Rose, leaving Landra in the long white room alone with Anson dePaul.

The sound of life-giving air whistling through the silver tube filled the room, filled her mind. Could she ever forget the sound of Anson's tortured breathing, the sight of Hollis plunging that shining knife into his throat; the sudden jarring knowledge that Adam's hand was seriously impaired, that he might not ever again be able to help a man like Anson? She forced herself to look into Anson's face, forced herself to imagine what he might have looked like before.

It was his eyes that made the difference. He opened them, and she looked straight into their dark depths. It was, quite suddenly, as though the ruined face did not exist, only the man. Anson dePaul the man was, and had always been, in his eyes. But Landra saw something in those eyes now that spoke to her heart as surely as though he had been able to utter the words: need, pure and simple; the same need Hollis had recognized in her. There was no thought of her earlier failure, only the irresistible urge to share what she knew to be the truth with Anson dePaul. Softly she said, "Did . . . did you hear me singing to Jimmy that night we were alone here?"

Almost imperceptibly he nodded, his eyes never moving from hers.

"It's true, you know."

Once more that small nod.

Slowly she placed a hand on his shoulder, forgetting, in her longing to communicate with him, her past feelings of fear, of revulsion. "He does love Jimmy, and Jesus loves you, too, so much that He died for you. All you have to do is accept that love. Do you, Anson?" Breathlessly, she watched him; it seemed an eon before she saw his head move affirmatively yet again. Her eyes stung with unshed tears as she stood by his side, wishing she could do more, knowing there was no more she could do.

After a long, quiet time she saw him try to speak. Though the tube prevented him from saying it, somehow she knew what he wanted of her. She began to sing, and her usually weak voice was different, beautiful.

"Jesus loves me, this I know. . . ." By the time she finished, the lovely clear sound of the simple words echoed round the room. Simple the words may have been, and childlike, but they were infinitely wise and full of meaning for the mortally ill man on the table before her. She knew with absolute assurance what had happened; the same miraculous thing that had happened to her with Hollis in his carriage, and to millions of others who heard and then believed. Anson believed . . . Anson belonged to the Christ she sang of. Her heart, so heavy and full of pain just a short time before, soared with the certain knowledge that he was safe now, whatever happened to his shattered body. And Anson dePaul knew it too. It showed in his eyes.

CHAPTER 16

It was very late when Landra awakened; the midmorning sun was bright and hot on her face. The first thought that occurred to her was of Anson—had he lived through that horrible ordeal last night? She hastily poured water from the pale blue china pitcher into its matching bowl and splashed it onto her face. It helped somewhat, and gave her the heart to comb through the tangled mass of dark red hair that lay heavy on her shoulders.

If only she could put on something cooler. With a slight tremor of rebellion, she walked quickly to the wardrobe and took out a white, full-sleeved blouse and black skirt. *So much for the confining custom of deep mourning*, she thought. After all, isn't it the heart that counts?

The dimity blouse seemed almost indecently light, even with its high, tight collar and billowy sleeves. With some difficulty she managed to do up the back buttons, and let the long, full skirt down over her head. There was no mirror, but a quick look over her shoulder made her glad she had the nerve not to wear those ridiculous bustles that were, she hoped, on the way out of the fashion scene.

In the kitchen she found Rose sitting at the table with a cup of tea before her. "Rose! How is Anson? Is he—"

Rose smiled gravely at the anxious look on Landra's face. "No thanks to me, he's better this morning. They're both with him now, Jimmy and Dr. Jarrett. I . . . I did stay with him some last night, after you went up, after the new young doctor left."

At the mention of Hollis, Landra felt a rush of gladness and she smiled encouragingly at Rose. "Don't blame yourself. I couldn't do it, either."

Still distressed she had not been able to help Anson when he had so desperately needed it, Rose repeated, "And I stayed with Anson after you left. Now sit down, and I'll get you some tea. You look like you could use some." She reached into the cupboard and took down a cup and saucer. Before she spoke again she stared for a long moment at the delicate cup. "Landra, I want you to know I keep the dishes for the three of us—Anson, Jimmy and me—completely separate from yours. And I always use a strong disinfectant on everything."

Landra met her pleading blue eyes. "I'm sure you take every precaution, Rose. And Adam has assured me it's only mildly contagious."

"Do you believe him?" Rose was watching her closely.

"Why, I . . . I don't have much choice, do I, if I insist on staying here?"

Rose said nothing more as she poured boiling water into a teapot and set it before Landra.

By the time Adam came into the kitchen, Landra was feeling much stronger, strong enough to ask if she could look in on Anson. His answer was short, and she could tell that although he, too, looked stronger, he was preoccupied. "I suppose. I've got to check him first, but I'm going into town right away, to see Rob."

"May I go?" Landra was eager to see the baby again.

He frowned, and said slowly, "I'm not certain that would be wise."

"But why not?"

"After that scene in Noirville yesterday, can you ask such a question? The lines are drawn now, and it might be very dangerous for anyone they think is on our side."

"But why must there be sides, with people divided and set against each other?" Landra asked passionately.

"Because we have differences of opinion," answered Adam. "That's oversimplifyng the problem, I know, but it happens to be true."

"Maybe it would be better if you did stay here, Landra," Rose ventured to say.

"No, I want to see Rob, and I'd also like to visit the Chaumonts and tell them that—" She hesitated as Adam's eyes searched her face keenly, then went on, "I want them to know I'm all right, and what's been happening here. I owe them that, Adam; they've been so kind to me."

"Perhaps you're right," he agreed. "Well, I must leave soon, as soon as we make sure Anson is holding on."

"That's all he's likely to do, isn't it?" said Rose, her voice soft and sad.

"Don't give up hope, Rose; we'll beat this thing." Adam tugged at the white sling on his arm, and a flash of pain crossed his face.

"Your arm—"

"It's fine, Landra. You go on to the lab to see Anson, and I'll be there shortly." His manner was firm; she didn't dare say anything further as he turned and left the room.

Anson no longer lay on the long, high table in the center of the laboratory. He was on the cot in the far corner, and it was Jimmy who sat beside him, an improvised black mask covering his eyes against the brightness of the sunlight filtering through the dark curtain. He turned toward her as he heard the door softly open and close. "Who is it?"

"It's Landra, Jimmy. Is Anson sleeping?"

"Yes," he whispered. "Just now he drifted off again. He's afraid he won't be able to finish his precious book. I can't think why anyone would want to read about us, but he says if they *knew*, things would be different. And he keeps trying to call for her."

"Who?"

"Marie . . . Marie . . . I see his mouth aching to form the word until I think it will drive me crazy."

"Marie was my mother's name."

"It's his wife's name, too. Except," he added, "she's not his wife anymore."

"What do you mean? Did she die?"

"Die!" The word was like an oath bursting from Jimmy's lips. The man on the cot stirred and Jimmy said, more quietly, "No, she didn't die. But because she believed *he* had, and by his own hand, too, she has remarried, and just this month gave birth to a son. His little daughter Suzanne was very dear to him, but like most of us, Anson wanted a son. He'll never have a son . . . *I'll never have a son* . . ."

He groaned, then gave a short, bitter laugh. "His wife thinks he committed suicide, that he drowned himself in the Mississippi River. And the horrible irony is, even now he clings to the miserable bit of life left to him with the strength of a hundred men. Even now, he doesn't want to die—"

Jimmy spoke of the man before him, but the words were for himself as well. Landra could only watch, her heart torn, as Jimmy reached, felt for its edge, and tenderly pulled the blanket up just short of the fearsome tube through which quietly whistled life-giving air into Anson's lungs. Jimmy's next words were spoken so softly she had to step closer to hear.

"Something Anson said once sticks in my mind . . . something about how dying wouldn't be so bad if it didn't take so long." His voice broke a little, then he said, "If only there was a chance to live . . . we aren't living, just a long time dying!"

A long time dying. Landra stared helplessly at the two men who must fight Death until it bore them, still struggling, away. At that moment, she wanted to fight for them, with them. How, she didn't know; but there had to be a way.

"Jimmy, I—" He raised his head and she went hesitantly on, "Jimmy, if you'll let me I'll sit with Anson when I get back. I want to help."

He nodded, not asking, as she half expected, *Why?* Perhaps he knew far better than she. Adam came in then, and she left to allow him to examine Anson in private.

Outside the day was bright and hot, and she stood and breathed deeply and gratefully, terribly aware that Anson had to fight for every breath. She let her eyes feast on the sunshine, which was only agony to Jimmy. She had so much, and they so little.

When Adam came out he helped her into the carriage. "This whole experience has been very difficult for you, I know, and I'm sorry."

"There's nothing you can do to make things any different, Adam. I know you would if you could. And now that I'm aware of the true situation, I only want to help."

He clucked to the horse and the carriage moved slowly down the oyster-shell drive under the protective shade of the tall pine trees. "You sound like your idealistic suitor, young Dr. Freman."

"He's just as sincere as I am, Adam Jarrett, and it seems to me as though you'd better accept help when it's offered!" Landra bit her lip; that was the old, impetuous Landra talking. Evidently she was not done with her, Landra thought wryly. She took a deep breath and said, "Really, Adam, you're going to need all of us. Anson and Jimmy and Rose, and others like them, are going to need all the champions they can get."

"You're right, of course. I'm sorry, Landra." His breath exhaled in a long sigh. "I seem to be saying that a lot lately. But it doesn't make anything different."

"Oh, Adam, don't get . . ." She started to say *discouraged,* but she realized he was already discouraged, and there wasn't much she could say to lift his spirits. Instead, she put her hand on his good arm and said softly, "We're in it with you now, Adam, and we're going to fight with you." In her heart a prayer began; a prayer for Adam and those they'd left behind in her childhood home—a prayer for herself that God would give wisdom and strength and patience.

At Carrie's, both the baby and the young woman who'd cared for him so faithfully were delighted to see Adam. Landra thought with pity that Carrie still hoped Adam would someday return her love. But Adam would most likely never love a woman again, Landra thought; he had room in his heart and mind only for the grim battle. She held the squirming, smiling baby out to Adam, who hugged him close, then gave him to Landra.

Rob took one look at Landra and set up a howl. "Here," said Carrie, "let me have him." She started to take the child from Landra with the same possessive air she'd shown before, but Adam shook his head.

"No, Carrie, leave him with her. I have something I want to tell you, and it's important." He drew her to the far side of the room, and Landra's fairly successful attempts to placate the baby prevented her from hearing anything but snatches of what they were saying.

It soon became apparent, however, that they disagreed, for Adam raised his voice enough so that Landra heard him say, "No matter what happens, you are to put the safety of the child first!"

"But, Adam, if you—"

"There is no earthly way for me to determine the outcome of that meeting, and I'm going to depend on you to see that he's kept safe. Is that clear?"

"Yes, of course." Carrie looked at Landra, dismayed that she should hear Adam speak to her in such a way. Adam came over to where Landra sat holding the baby and took him from her, holding the curly, dark head close to his face for a long moment, his eyes shut. Carrie came and took Rob before he could hand him back to Landra.

Adam, his gaze still on the child, said, "If I don't get back

... as soon as I hope, remember what I told you."

"I will, Adam, I will." Carrie's eyes held a silent plea for him to say something more.

He took her hand for a moment, then said gently, "Try not to worry, Carrie, all right?" Then he walked to the door, opened it, and stood waiting for Landra. "I must go and speak to Dr. Freman. Would you prefer to stay here or go with me now?"

"I'll go," said Landra. Carrie Chaumont's hostility was almost palpable in the small, homey room. Landra retrieved little Rob, hugged and kissed him, then gave him up with reluctance. Carrie stood at the door watching them drive away, Landra was certain.

As they neared the Freman house Adam, who had been very quiet during the drive, said, "I'm going to ask that Dr. Freman stay at the house with Anson and Jimmy while you, Lucas, and I go to the council meeting. I've nothing but instinct to go on, but he seems to be just what he says he is. And if you trust him ..."

"I certainly do." Hesitantly, she asked, "Why do you want me to go, Adam? I'm perfectly willing, even eager, because I feel it could answer a great many of my questions. I just wondered why you want me."

"It's simple, really. If you, having lost your sister to Hansen's disease, are living in the same house with others who are also stricken, if you are obviously standing by me and my colleagues, it could lend strength to our arguments. And as you so aptly pointed out, we need all the help we can get."

"I see," she nodded. "Of course I'll go. And I'm sure Hollis will stay at Greenlea."

When Hollis heard Adam's request, he hardly allowed him to finish before he assured him he would do as he asked. Once Adam's mission was accomplished, he told Landra he had other things to attend to, and quite simply said that Hollis could see her home. Then, without waiting for a reply, he left.

For a moment Hollis gazed at Landra, and she at him; both were overcome by an unfamiliar shyness. Then Hollis smiled broadly, that lock of fair hair dangling over his forehead, and held out his arms to her. She flew to him, so glad for their sheltering that she felt the sting of tears. When he lifted her chin and saw that her eyes were brimming, he said, "Landra, my love, what is it?"

She gave in to the impulse to smooth back his hair; it was

as soft and fine as Rob's. Landra's hand moved gently to his ear, then his jaw. "Nothing . . . nothing . . . I'm just so happy to be safe in your arms!"

"Then I'll never let you go," he murmured against her hair, holding her even closer. "I hated leaving you last night, to face all that alone."

She smiled up at him. "Aren't you the one who told me I'd never be alone now? That He's always with me—"

He stopped her with a kiss, a long but gentle kiss that made her legs weak, her breath short. "I did, indeed, tell you that. But I want to be with you, too, to shield you from pain and trouble."

She bent her head and laid it on his chest. Her voice was muffled as she said, "I'm afraid no one, not even you, can do that for me. I find that their pain is . . . is my pain; I feel it with them."

"Ah, Landra, that's how He is with His children. He loves us and feels our pain."

"Oh, then why doesn't He take it away?" she cried out. "I don't understand!"

"Neither do I, love, neither do I. But I trust Him, and that's the best we can do when we don't understand."

She held him tightly for a long while, struggling with her tears again, conquering them finally. "Hollis, you seem so far ahead of me; you seem to know so much more."

"You keep thinking that." He chuckled. "If I'm to be the head of our household and you're to look up to me, it's best if you think I'm superior!"

"Oh, you're joking again," she said in mock despair. "Be serious." Then she looked up into his face and said softly, "On second thought, don't stop joking; it makes things more bearable." The shyness struck her again at the thought of being a part of his home. "I hadn't really imagined it, you know."

"What's that?"

"You, and me, and . . . and a home together." Wonderingly she saw the look in his intense blue eyes.

"Then let's imagine it. We'll draw up some plans, and build our dream house in our imaginations. Dreams are just the first step, you know, to reality."

"Reality." She took a deep breath. "Reality is back at Greenlea, Hollis, those three and others like them, and needs so enormous I can't begin to imagine."

"That is true, Landra. But reality is also the fact that I love you and you love me, and that in the midst of all this pain and horror we found each other, and together we can face anything." He gazed into her eyes, so long that Landra felt the moment might go on forever; she was content to let it. But he murmured finally, "I'd best get you to the Chaumont's. Mrs. Olsen is due back from the market, and she already thinks I've compromised you."

"Are you sure she doesn't think it's I who's compromised you?" Landra teased.

"Possibly," he agreed with a grin.

At the Chaumont house the three little girls were in the yard, in an elaborate playhouse made of sticks laid out on the smooth packed dirt. There were several dolls in various stages of dress and undress; the three little mothers stopped suddenly, interrupting their maternal conversation as they saw Landra.

"It's Miss Cole!" Jeannette smiled shyly as Landra stepped down. "Have you come to see Mama?"

"Yes, but to see you, too," answered Landra. She offered her hand to the little girl, then looked back at Hollis. In a whisper she said to him, "Look, they've got their dream house laid out. Do you suppose we could—" She flashed a brilliant smile at the adoring look on his face, then tried to assume a more serious expression as Rene Chaumont came onto the porch.

"Landra!" She came out, hands extended, and took Landra's in her own, her welcoming smile encompassing Hollis. "I was hoping you would come by. I've been awfully worried since you were here last." As the three of them stepped into the front room, Landra saw with a shock that Katy sat beside Denis on the sofa.

With a strangled cry the blond girl sprang to her feet. "You didn't tell me *she* was coming! I don't want to be in the same house with her!"

"Kathryn! Stop that at once!" Rene's sharp words seemed to have little effect on Katy.

Denis merely rolled his eyes and shrugged his shoulders as he pulled the agitated girl down beside him. "Now, Katy, you're behaving terribly. Miss Landra will think you're—"

"What do I care what she thinks of me? After what's in the paper she's the one that ought to care what *we* think!" She grabbed the newspaper that lay on the table at the end of the sofa. "It's all right here . . ." She trailed off as Denis took her arm firmly and lifted her up as he stood.

"Please excuse us, Landra. Katy and I, we've got some talking to do." His smile was forced, and Landra was embarrassed for him.

"Of course, Denis. It's all right, really it is." Landra's quiet words had no calming effect on Katy, who started to speak again as Denis pulled her almost bodily out of the room. However, she stopped him at the door and threw the newspaper at Landra.

Obviously troubled and concerned for Landra, Hollis had said nothing. He leaned against the wall, having declined Rene's offer of a chair, and watched Landra's face carefully as she read.

The headlines were much the same as before, and she scanned the lines below. When she came to the section pertaining to the upcoming council meeting, she slowly read aloud:

> Dr. Isodore Dyer, eminent dermatologist and champion of the proposed leprosarium, will be aided by Dr. Adam Jarrett, who has been harboring and treating three lepers in his own home, Greenlea, unbeknownst to his friends and neighbors. Dr. Dyer reports he and Dr. Jarrett will present conclusive evidence that the proposed "hospital" will be of inestimable value to the area.
>
> However, the opponents of such an undertaking have clearly stated they will refute any arguments that are made, and that they have spokesmen who will make clear beyond all doubt which course of action we, as a city, should take. These spokesmen, among the most respected members of the medical profession in this area . . ."

Landra's eyes met Hollis' steady gaze in a flash of intuition. "They wanted you to be among them?"

His flat statement sobered her even further. "Yes, I think so. It would have been almost as good as having my grandfather. The irony is, he would probably have been with them. Although I'm not certain—"

"Don't be," Rene cut in with a grave, warning look. "Your grandfather is an honest, fair man, and I choose to believe he'd have done what is right, right for us all. I think he'd be proud of your stand."

"Mrs. Chaumont, I appreciate your confidence, but surely you know most of your friends and neighbors don't share it."

"I know. And I'm not saying I'm not afraid, afraid for my

girls, for myself and Denis. But I just can't go along with this craziness, either. Some of these folks I've known all my life, and they were out there acting like crazy people."

"Hysteria is a frightening thing," acknowledged Hollis.

"More scary to me than . . . than whatever is out at Greenlea," said Rene, a courageous smile on her face. "Whatever I can do to help, I will."

Landra went to her and put her arms around the woman, hugging her tightly. "You can't know what it means to have you here, and saying these things. It makes me feel better, safer, as though the whole world isn't insane, after all."

Rene laughed shyly. "I'm not much protection. But you get me riled up, or let someone threaten one of those little fillies out there, and watch out!"

"Landra," Hollis broke in. "I hate to take you away, but we'd really best be going. I want to ask Adam exactly what to do about Anson and the others."

Landra pulled away from her friend's embrace. "You're right. I'm ready." To Rene she said, "There aren't enough words—"

"Don't try. Just let me know how things go. And—" She hesitated, then said, "Don't let that awful little scene with Katy bear on your mind, you hear?"

"I won't." Landra followed Hollis out, said her good-byes to the little girls, and they set out for Greenlea. Just as they pulled into the oyster-shell drive, they heard the sound of another carriage, and saw Adam as he reined over a team of two horses, which were pulling a carriage far larger than the one he had let Landra take before.

Adam stepped out of the carriage, a folded newspaper clutched in his hand. "Have you seen this?" he asked, the anger in his voice barely controlled.

Hollis nodded. "It doesn't specifically name anyone." He helped Landra down and the three of them walked to the shaded veranda.

"They've got several, I'll wager. Poor, deluded men who'll do what they're told, say all the 'right' things, never realizing the outrageous damage they're doing with their lies!"

"But, Adam," said Landra, "you said yourself there are two sides; perhaps it will strengthen your position if all the facts are known."

"They don't have the facts. Only stupid, nonsensical lies. It's a case of the most blatant prejudice, and there is no defense against prejudice except the truth. We can only hope they'll listen." His shoulders slumped suddenly, and Landra could see the deep lines of fatigue and worry creasing his face. Just when she was about to speak, he said, "The only trouble is, prejudice is almost always stone deaf."

Landra wanted badly to say something that would lift his spirits and encourage him. It was Hollis, however, who said, "If we're right, sir, and I believe we are, then somehow we'll win."

The quiet conviction in his tone made Adam look at him keenly. "I hope so, Dr. Freman. I certainly hope so." He moved slowly away, down the veranda, and sat in a chair, one hand over his eyes.

Left alone, Hollis bent and quickly kissed Landra, who, though she felt a momentary shyness, put her arms around him and held him tight for a moment. "Oh, Hollis, I'm afraid."

"Don't be," he murmured against her cheek. "I really believe what I told Dr. Jarrett."

She drew back. "And you believe they will be successful at the council meeting, that the hospital will be allowed at Elkhorn, and they can help Rose and Jimmy and—"

"Whoa!" He laughed softly. "I didn't say that, though I certainly hope so." He put an arm around her waist and began walking back to his buggy. "I guess what I meant was that we will continue the fight for what we believe in, that ultimately we will win." He shook his head in wonder. "Will you listen to me? A few weeks ago I wasn't even aware of the situation; now I count myself as a willing participant in the battle."

"Ultimately we'll win," Landra repeated. "I only hope it won't be too late for Anson."

"So do I." He stopped at the buggy. "Well, I'm glad of one thing. They've stopped running me off—Dr. Jarrett and Dr. Delacroix!" He kissed her once more, and stepped up into the buggy. "I may not see you before the meeting."

"Why not?"

Hollis looked pleased at the chagrin on her face. "There are a lot of things about the whole situation I don't know, and I definitely need that knowledge. Also, I need to visit my grandfather."

"I . . . I'll miss you." His only answer before he drove away was a smile, but it warmed her; she knew what he was thinking.

Slowly she made her way to Adam and sank into the chair beside him.

"He seems to be a fine young man."

"Yes, he is, Adam." They were both quiet for a time; then Landra said, "Where was Sam'l this morning? I didn't see him."

"He's gone."

"Gone? Where, and why?"

"I sent him over to act as a sort of lookout at Elkhorn." He shook his head. "For such a smart woman, Landra, you sometimes overlook the obvious. Staying at Greenlea last night almost finished the old man."

Stung by his words, she said, "I'm not sure I know what you mean."

"I mean he only stayed because you bewitched him with those green eyes and played on his loyalty to me; he would have gladly flown the coop right away. I found him up this morning at dawn, sitting and shivering on the veranda here. I think he was just about to leave anyway, no matter what his conscience said, so I asked him to go over to Elkhorn and watch for trouble. He was glad for the opportunity to leave honorably, as well as to do something useful."

"But couldn't that be dangerous?"

"He won't show himself, and he has a horse and instructions to come to Greenlea at once if there's any sign of trouble."

"Adam, I'm sorry I persuaded Sam'l to stay. It seemed the right thing to do at the time." Her eyes begged him to understand.

"I know you meant well. You're just impetuous; you can't help being what you are," he said, not unkindly. A look of consternation showed suddenly on his face. "And I can't seem to help being forgetful. I meant to discuss Anson and Jimmy with Dr. Freman. Well, perhaps there'll be time when—" Just then Lucas came out of the house, and the two men were immediately immersed in talk about Anson's condition.

He was better, it seemed. Landra followed them into the house and listened to the flow of medical jargon about the likelihood of Anson's recovery. He was better. That one fact, gleaned from the conversation, was enough to lighten her heart. Somehow Anson had become vitally important to her. If only something could be done for Jimmy, something to save his eyes.

Landra went slowly up to her room; uppermost in her mind was the thought of how much easier and better it would be if Rose and Anson and Jimmy were in a proper hospital, with the facilities to help, if not cure, their ravaged bodies.

CHAPTER 17

It was late, perhaps almost twelve, when Landra finally gave up trying to sleep and rose from her tangled bed. She drew on her wrapper, lit a lamp, and stepped out into the dark hall. There were many things on her mind, not the least of which was the baby, Rob. If an attempt to establish the hospital at Elkhorn were successful, there was no reason why she couldn't care for the child here, at Greenlea. There must be ways of cleaning a place, of sanitizing it and making it safe against the danger of the disease.

She felt drawn to the nursery. The thought of Bethany, her unbearable sadness, the endless hours she must have spent grieving here smote Landra. Sitting in the rocker, a soft blue blanket in her hand, she whispered a vow: "I'll love him for you, Beth. It won't be the same, but I'll love him and take care of him like you would have wanted." The tears flowed silently, unknowingly down her face.

A small sound at the door made her look up to see Adam standing there. "I saw you come in." He walked over to where she sat, and stood for a long moment, his eyes taking in the room as though he had not seen it before. "I haven't been in here since Bethany died. She used to spend endless hours in that rocker where you're sitting, with tears on her face." He reached down and brushed the tears from Landra's cheeks, then took the blue blanket from her, stroking its softness with his thumb. "It was never my plan to have a child. After Dyer confirmed the diagnosis of Hansen's disease, I swore there'd be no child, even if I could never touch her again. But . . ."

He stopped, and Landra searched his face. To see his look of pain and longing hurt her. But she knew somehow that he had a great need to speak of his pain; instinctively she knew he had not shared it with anyone. Gently she encouraged him. "She's in your thoughts a great deal, isn't she?"

He nodded. "Bethany was a very beautiful woman; she was always irresistible enough to me just . . . doing nothing. Then she made up her mind that she was going to give me a child, to make up for losing her. And I—God help me—I wasn't man enough to deny myself!"

"Oh, Adam—"

He ignored her and continued, his voice dull. "She was absolutely certain she could have the child and then give it up. During her confinement she was happy, convinced she was strong enough to do what she had set out to do. But when the time came, we both found out how terribly impossible it was. I even thought it would have been far better had she miscarried, like all the other times. But Rob was a beautiful, healthy, full-term infant. Ironic, isn't it?" He stopped, a faraway, dazed expression on his face.

"There were times when I was afraid for the sanity of us both; she cried and begged for him for weeks after I took him away." In the dimness of the room she could see the pain in his eyes. "You understand, don't you—I had to take him away, or he would have almost certainly been infected. You understand, don't you?"

"Of course, Adam." Landra tried to speak soothingly. "There was nothing else you could do."

"She calmed somewhat after a while. But she was never the same. I only wanted to comfort her, to help her; but every move I made she interpreted as one she must avoid at all costs. Repeatedly she told me never again would she go through that, even if it meant we could never be—" He cleared his throat, then said, very slowly, "It was all my fault. If I had restrained myself, made sure she hadn't gotten pregnant, she might still be alive now."

"Adam, how can you say that? Bethany did what she did because she loved you! What's done is done, and can you say it was all for nothing? If you do, that means her love was wasted, and her life, her very life, was wasted."

"I'm not denying she loved me; in a way she died for me. But it would have meant immeasurably more if she had loved me enough to live for me."

They were both silent for a time; then Landra broke the

silence by saying, "Adam, what can I do? Just tell me, and I will . . . anything."

"There's nothing, except to be present and obviously sympathetic at the council meeting tomorrow night." He looked at her closely. "You are sympathetic, aren't you? You do believe in the hospital?"

"Yes, of course. The last couple of days have convinced me, and I'll do whatever I can. But—" She hesitated. There was a sense of closeness, of ease between the two of them that had not been present before. It wouldn't do to jeopardize it now.

"But what, Landra?" asked Adam anxiously, afraid her hesitation had something to do with the hospital project.

"I was thinking, before you came in, about Rob. Would it be possible to disinfect the house, make it safe for him to live here if Anson and the others are at Elkhorn?"

"Yes, I think so," Adam answered, still uncertain as to her intent.

"I'd like nothing better than to take care of him, here. I think Bethany would be pleased." When he didn't answer, she said, "Adam, I'm sorry about accusing you of being responsible for Beth's sickness. Please, let me make it up to you."

"That's not necessary."

"But it is! Carrie Chaumont has done a good job, I'm sure, but Rob is my own flesh and blood. Oh, Adam, I'd love him as though he were my own."

Troubled, he said, "Carrie has loved and cared for him just like that, as if he were her own. I owe a great debt to her. I don't know how I'd have gotten through the last year without her. She's been wonderful with Rob, and she's in complete sympathy with the project."

Landra started to protest, then changed her mind. There would be plenty of time to make arrangements later, when they knew the outcome of the council meeting. Briefly, she marveled at the change in her; she knew that before her experience with Christ, she would most likely have argued with Adam and insisted on having her own way. *Thank you, Lord . . . I did ask for patience.* Aloud she said, "I'm glad someone who cares has been with him, and—"

Rose pushed open the door then, almost beside herself with anxiety. "Dr. Jarret, please excuse me, but it's Jimmy. Please come!"

"Yes, of course, Rose, right away." To Landra he said, "I'll be quite busy tomorrow. If I don't see you before then, can you be ready to leave for the council meeting at six o'clock, no later?"

"Yes, Adam, I will." After they left, she sat for a long time in the little rocker before she returned to her room, thinking about the future, wondering what it held for them all.

The next morning, true to his word, Adam was not to be found. Landra took Rose's place and helped apply the hot compresses to Jimmy's eyes for a time, and watched in unwilling fascination as Lucas changed the inner tube in the cannula which delivered the life-giving air to Anson's lungs.

"How long will he need the tube?" she asked.

"Until he can breathe comfortably if it is plugged," answered Lucas. He quickly and efficiently went about his work. "If only we had the hospital; there's so much more we could do for them."

"Yes," Landra agreed. "I can see that. Do you believe that Elkhorn is the best location, Lucas?"

"I most certainly do," he said. "Adam told me your young doctor has decided to join us." He carefully adjusted the tape on Anson's throat, then laid a reassuring hand on his shoulder. "We are going to need good men when we get the hospital equipped. When I think of it . . . tonight is going to be the culmination of a very crucial time."

"I pray it will go in our favor."

"It's going to take more than prayers." He turned from Anson and looked Landra straight in the eye. "I hope you realize what you've let yourself in for. You'd be better off if you'd pack up and go back to New York."

"There's certainly nothing for me there!" Landra's temper flared momentarily; then she calmed and said, "I have faith that God will give me whatever I need. Strength, or courage, or—"

"Well, I hope you're right," he said abruptly. "Please excuse me, I must check the supplies we'll be leaving for Dr. Freman."

Landra tried to smile, and murmured something about needing to get some air as she left the lab. She walked down to the meadow and sat with her back to one of the huge old oak trees. The small stone that marked Bethany's grave was near, and her thoughts as she gazed at it were directed to it . . . or to the lost sister beneath it. The air was warm and there was harldy any breeze, yet it was pleasant under the shade of the trees. She plucked absently at the little flowers growing all around. *We'll do the best we can, Bethany . . . we'll fight the good fight.*

CHAPTER 18

Landra dressed carefully that evening, as if she were going to a party instead of a meeting which could drastically alter her life, not to mention the lives of those three downstairs and many others like them. She and Rose had sponged the black silk and pressed it until it looked presentable once more. She placed the black hat with its little backward feather wings on her head, fanned the fine mist of veil over her face. The pale face reflected in the mirror betrayed her inner agitation. She pinched her cheeks and bit her lips until they stung, then decided she was as ready as she'd ever be.

Downstairs there was no sign of either Adam or Lucas. It was Rose who came to stand beside her.

"How is Anson this evening, Rose, and Jimmy?"

Rose's eyes filled with tears. "Anson is pretty much the same. But Jimmy, my poor Jimmy!" She choked as the sobs rose in her throat.

Alarmed, Landra said, "What's wrong . . . something new?"

"No, it's his eyes, I'm afraid his sight is almost gone, and he's awfully bitter." Her thin shoulders shook as she covered her own eyes with both hands.

Landra tried desperately to think of some words of comfort, something. "Rose, didn't Dr. Jarrett, or Lucas, perhaps, tell me there would be no more pain after . . . when Jimmy can no longer see?" Rose nodded but did not look at Landra, who went on gently. "If there's no help for the blindness, wouldn't it be some comfort to you if he's free from that terrible pain?"

Rose took her hands away. "Yes, but . . ."

"But what? You can help him, be his eyes, couldn't you?"

"If we stay here. But he'll be alone if we have to go there."

Landra frowned, not certain about the girl's meaning. "Surely Dr. Dyer and Adam would allow you to help Jimmy when the new hospital at Elkhorn is established, Rose. I know they would."

"Maybe," said Rose softly. "But if they won't let us stay at Elkhorn, we'll all have to go to Indian Camp, and *there* they won't! Fences and walls and worlds will separate me from my Jimmy! The men and women are never allowed to be together, not even to talk, and . . . and even if they wanted to, *no one is allowed to marry*!" A fresh paroxysm of sobs shook her, and Landra stood by helplessly. She was relieved when Adam came through the front door, followed closely by Hollis.

Though she was glad to see Hollis, it was to Adam that she spoke. "Adam, Rose has been telling me about Indian Camp! Can it really be as bad as she says?"

"I'm afraid so. But it's the best we have to offer unless we're successful tonight. Are you ready to leave?" Without waiting for her to reply he said to Rose, "I'll check on Jimmy one last time. Don't worry, Rose, I'll take care of him, wherever we are." Landra was touched by his gentleness as he led the girl down the hall, murmuring words of reassurance. Dimly she noticed his arm was not bound by the sling.

Hollis had stood quietly aside, and now he said, "I know Dr. Jarrett feels Anson and Jimmy need medical supervision at all times, but I can't help but be concerned about you. If things don't go well at the council meeting, it could be dangerous." He clasped her hand tightly. "Feelings are running high, Landra, and the crowd could get out of hand again. I'm not sure it's wise for you to go—"

He was interrupted by Adam, who came striding down the hall. "They're all three in the lab, Dr. Freman. I believe you know what to do. I appreciate your willingness to help."

Hollis gave Landra one last searching look, but he said nothing more of his fears, just squeezed her hand. "Don't worry about them. I'll see they're well taken care of. Glad to be useful for a change."

Adam nodded, and they could see his mind was racing ahead to the battle before them. "Lucas is bringing the carriage around, Landra; don't be long," he said as he left.

For a moment they stood just looking at each other; then Landra said softly, "I'm glad you're here with them, Hollis." She planted a swift, light kiss on his cheek and followed Adam out, knowing he was impatiently waiting.

It was dusk as Lucas, Landra, and Adam drove up to the ferry which would carry them across the river to the winking lights of the crescent city. When she asked about the larger carriage, Adam replied that although it was probably totally unnecessary, he had decided it would do no harm to be prepared in the event that all those at Greenlea might need to leave at once. At her anxious question as to whether or not he anticipated serious trouble, he became even more evasive. She realized he was only trying to spare her worry, but she thought in exasperation that not knowing only made her worry more.

When they reached the city Landra marveled at the difference between it and most of the neighboring small towns and cities. While they were sleepily rolling up their sidewalks and closing for the night, New Orleans was like a giant, fragrant, night flower just beginning to open and spread its gay, gaudy petals to the sultry evening.

The horses' hoofs rang out on the brick street, and Landra looked eagerly for some name, some remembrance. But it had been so long ago, and there were other things on her mind which canceled out whatever enjoyment she might feel at reliving childhood memories. The crowd of people outside the building where the council meeting was to be held was quite large, and their mood reminded her vividly of the ugly mob in Noirville. There were raucous cries from newsboys, shouting the vitriolic contents of the stacks of papers they carried.

"Extra! Extra! Read all about it! New Orleans in danger of the terrible scourge—the leper plague!"

Adam exploded. "That's grossly unfair! How can we expect a just hearing before the council when the public has been exposed to such ignorant, superstitious accusations? I thought newspapers were supposed to be impartial reporters of news, not instruments to prejudice the people before a trial even begins!"

"Easy, Dr. Jarrett," said Lucas. "It's not a trial, after all."

"Isn't it? Aren't we all, doctors and patients alike, on trial for our lives? Well, we're going to be acquitted of the crime of being ill, and of trying to cure that illness," he finished harshly. "Do you hear? *We're going to win!*"

"Of course we are, Adam," said Landra, putting every shred of confidence she could muster into her voice, when she actually was watching the crowd anxiously, hoping against hope they wouldn't be recognized as they entered the building.

She was spared, however, for Lucas drove past the front entrance around to the rear, where he got out and tied the horses securely to the railing. Quickly, as if he, too, shared Landra's fears, Adam helped her out and the three of them slipped into the building. The narrow hallway through which they hurriedly walked was deserted, but when they stepped into the large room Landra was dismayed at the crowded, smoke-filled atmosphere. She scanned the crowd, recognizing vaguely a couple of the men who had been present at Greenlea a few days ago . . . and Dr. Lardbelly. She stifled a nervous bubble of laughter. Really, she must ask Adam his name.

There was a long, narrow table at which several men already sat, though there were empty chairs as well. The thought occurred to her that Adam, she, and Lucas might possibly have to occupy those places. She looked up at the U-shaped balcony. It was full. The men were talking loudly, some waving cigars excitedly; from their seats they possessed an excellent view of the table below. The men on the lower floor spilled haphazardly out the big double front doors, blending with the angry crowd outside.

Once more she looked around the room and into the balcony above, confirming her earlier, disturbing conclusion. There was not another woman in the building. Adam had not told her it would be like this . . . but she was here, and lifted her chin bravely as a red-faced man, mopping his whiskered jowls with a huge white handkerchief, told the three of them to be seated at the highly visible table.

A ripple of remarks stirred among the men and she could hear fragments. ". . . his sister-in-law—do you suppose she's going to make a speech, too?"

Just then the man at the head of the table took a gavel in hand and pounded vigorously, demanding the attention of those present. Adam whispered, "That's Albert G. Phelps, who succeeded Dyer as president of the Board of Control. He called this meeting."

"Gentlemen! Gentlemen! May I have your attention, please!" The din had quieted, only to erupt again as Dr. Dyer came into the room and took his place beside Mr. Phelps.

"Gentlemen, we may now begin. As most of you know, the man seated on my right is Dr. Isodore Dyer, and on my left—"

But he was not to be allowed to continue, at least not for several moments. The angry outbursts of shouts and catcalls overrode his protests. This time it took Mr. Phelps quite a while of banging the gavel to calm them. Landra clenched her teeth. It was almost as if Mr. Phelps was a referee, and this was a boxing match. She could imagine him saying, "And on my right, the mighty John L. Sullivan, and his opponent . . ." The atmosphere might be suitable for a prize fight, she thought, but certainly not for the life-and-death matter that was to be decided.

Phelps persisted, and finally the noise of the crowd subsided into an angry buzz as he said, "On my left we have Drs. N. C. Stevens and Thomas Morely, who will represent the opposition."

Landra felt a rush of gladness that Hollis had not cast his lot with the opposition; she knew it would have made their love impossible. She could not imagine being without Hollis; he seemed to have always been a dear part of her heart.

There was no time for any more speculation. Mr. Phelps was saying, "Gentlemen, in order to present both sides of this issue, we are going to have to proceed at once, and not waste any more time. We must observe some rules, or chaos will reign and nothing will be accomplished. We will allow Dr. Stevens and Dr. Morely to begin, and in turn, give Dr. Dyer and his associates equal time to refute the arguments of the opposition." He ignored the angry outburst from several men in the balcony and calmly continued. "Do you agree this is a fair way to proceed, gentlemen?" He glanced around the table, and at the nods of assent, extended his hand to Dr. Stevens, who shook it, then rose to speak.

"Mr. Phelps, members of my learned profession, ma'am"—here he smiled slightly at Landra, who shrank from the scores of eyes turned on her and tried to smile back as he continued—"and all of you who have come here tonight in the interests of justice and—"

He was interrupted by several calls of "Get on with it! Say your piece!"

Dr. Stevens, a slight, balding man of perhaps forty, wiped his forehead carefully with his handkerchief and took a drink of water from a glass that sat on the table before him. "Yes, yes, of course. As I was saying, we are here to find and present the truth, for all to know."

Landra felt Adam stiffen, and knew he was on the verge of getting to his feet and interrupting Dr. Stevens. She slipped her hand under his arm and squeezed it lightly. When he met her eyes, she smiled. He gave an almost imperceptible nod, then relaxed a little. But his mouth was still set in a hard, unrelenting line as he heard Dr. Stevens' next words.

"Leprosy, or Hansen's disease, as Dr. Dyer would have us call it, is shrouded in the mists of antiquity. We doctors know little about it—exactly how it is transmitted, why it manifests itself in so many ghastly forms, and, most important, how to arrest it. I confess to you that I, like most of you here, with some exceptions, of course"—he glanced at Dr. Dyer with a derisive smile—"I know practically nothing of the disease."

"Then why in the name of heaven is he acting as the 'expert' for the opposition?" muttered Adam.

Evidently Dr. Stevens heard him, for he paused. But not for long, as he went on to say, "I am immensely thankful to be able to tell you that I have not seen a case of leprosy since I was a student in 1884. It was an experience I hope is not repeated in my lifetime. I feel very strongly that it is my duty to inform the populace of the extreme danger involved in locating a leprosarium so near a major city such as New Orleans."

From the crowd near the door there arose a loud chorus of agreement, some of the men stamping their feet and whistling.

"Please, please, there will be order, gentlemen, or I will adjourn this meeting until a later time!" Mr. Phelps banged furiously with his gavel and finally made himself understood, and evidently believed, for the men quieted. "You may go on, Dr. Stevens."

"Thank you." Once more Dr. Stevens nervously mopped at the shine of perspiration on his face, and with the air of a man about to shoot his final big gun, said loudly, "As I was saying, I think before the final decision is made, every concerned citizen should be aware that this foul disease is so contagious that the presence of a leper home would be a terrible menace to the neighborhood; it can be spread through the very atmosphere, quite possibly carried by mosquitoes and flies! Surely there are those among you who can recall the horror of yellow fever—perhaps." His voice lowered dramatically. "Perhaps many of you lost loved ones—lost them to the dread scourge of Yellow Jack!"

"Yes, yes!" There were cries of pained assent, and the men

in the hot, crowded room seemed to merge, at least in Landra's mind, into a menacing mob whose rage threatened to erupt like boiling lava from a volcano. She tightened her grip on Adam's arm, and was very glad to feel a slight pressure of response from him, although he did not speak or look at her. His rigid, stony expression was much like Dyer's; both men looked dangerously close to erupting themselves.

"And so, gentlemen," concluded Dr. Stevens passionately, "you cannot, you must not allow this madness to continue! Your women, your wives and daughters, your little sons . . . your very own healthy bodies would be threatened! I say we must stop, once and for all, those who would force this horrendous institution upon us. Thank you." Abruptly he sat down, as though the effort of speaking had drained him, as perhaps it had.

Mr. Phelps nodded to Dr. Morely, who stood slowly. He did not look at Landra and Adam as he began to speak. "Gentlemen, what I have to say is, in a way, of lesser importance than the issues of which my learned colleague Dr. Stevens has spoken. I realize lives are vastly more precious than financial concern. But that does not preclude the very real fact that if these men are allowed to turn Elkhorn plantation into a leprosarium, an asylum for those doomed to a living death, it will affect the lives of almost every citizen for many miles around."

There was a stillness, a silence in the room that had not been present before. Dazed by the implications of that silence, Landra looked at the faces of the men. Was it possible that the mere hint of a danger to that most vulnerable part of a man's anatomy, his pocketbook, could command such quiet stillness, attentive stillness? It would certainly seem so! The middle-aged doctor, who did not look very prosperous himself, continued.

"The value of your property would decrease sharply. Your neighbors, should you be brave enough to stay, would move away. And in another way, no less real, your homes and families would be seriously threatened. The presence of a leprosarium would be a grave detriment to each and every one of you, and halt progress of the thriving and wonderful city that we all love!" He allowed himself one quick defiant glance at Adam and Lucas as he finished. "Think long and hard before you make a decision that would affect every one of us for many years to come. I thank you for your kind attention. Mr. Phelps—" He sat down.

Mr. Phelps nodded gravely. It was a well-known fact he was

in sympathy with Dr. Dyer, but it was also known that he was a scrupulously fair man, and there was not a man in the room who did not, to a large degree, trust him and his ability to rule fairly. When he spoke now, there was a respectful lull in the conversation that had begun when Dr. Morely was finished.

"And now, we'll allow Dr. Dyer to speak. You will give him your respectful and undivided attention, I'm sure." But once more there were angry shouts as Dyer rose, this time from the crowd outside. Dr. Dyer patiently ignored them, and Mr. Phelps banged the gavel. Either the gavel or the table, Landra thought, might not last the night.

Dyer's face bore an alert, intense expression, and Landra felt instinctively that whatever he would say would be true and vital. "Gentlemen, and Miss Cole," he began. Landra acknowledged with a small smile. He went on. "First, I want to establish the fact that what Dr. Morely has intimated is not necessarily true. As most of you know, in the fall of 1898 several patients suffering from Hansen's disease were taken by river barge to Indian Camp, in Iberville Parish. Besides the crew, there were a number of newspapermen and myself, as well as the seven expatients of Dr. Beard."

"Yeah!" someone shouted, "they come from Dr. Beard's pesthouse down on Hagan Avenue!"

"The facilities at the house on Hagan Avenue, as well as the limited amount of time Dr. Beard was able to devote to them, made it a poor place for those harbored there," answered Dr. Dyer calmly. "They were left largely to their own devices, unfortunately."

"What about them that didn't go? I heard one of 'em stayed right here, over in Jefferson Parish. I heard that *he*"—the man who spoke pointed at Adam—"that he took 'em into his own home, and then his own wife died of leprosy!"

Landra drew in her breath sharply. Reason told her the man had been coached and planted specifically for the purpose of bringing Adam's part in the situation to light, but she couldn't help being terribly, terribly frightened.

"In a moment," said Dr. Dyer, "my friend and co-worker, Dr. Adam Jarrett, will be allowed to speak, and will explain his actions himself. But now, I will try to make clear to you what I began. In the years that Indian Camp plantation has housed the patients suffering from Hansen's disease, all fear and prejudice against it has died out in Iberville Parish, and no property has depreciated in value. On the contrary, the value of the ground rented by the board has actually increased from $10,000 to well over $14,000 since 1894. So you can see the basis of Dr. Morely's arguments are false." He looked pointedly at Morely, who refused to meet his steady gaze.

"Indeed," continued Dr. Dyer, "Whenever the true scientific facts are known, people are able to brush away the ignorance of centuries and accept the situation in its true reality. We must make an effort to do the only humane thing possible. The facilities at Indian Camp are so woefully lacking that we are, in all probability, sentencing some of the more seriously ill patients to an early death."

"Good! We're well rid of 'em!" a hoarse, ugly voice shouted.

"I'll choose to believe that the majority of you here tonight do not share that barbarian's opinion, that you want to see progress made for those unfortunate enough to be stricken with Hansen's disease. After all, gentlemen, we aren't in the Dark Ages any longer. This is 1901, and we are supposedly enlightened, well-informed men of medicine!"

He spoke with a quiet, deadly assurance, and no more outcries were heard. "The location of Indian Camp creates more problems than it solves. The geographical segregation of the patients is cruel and deliberate. It is over eighty miles from New Orleans, and a good twenty-five miles from Baton Rouge. Besides the river, there is only one access to the home, an extremely precarious pair of rutty tracks that can be called a dirt road only by courtesy, totally impassible in wet weather. There is no post office, no mail service except by haphazard arrangement. They are, for all practical purposes, cut off from the outside world."

His voice was strong, and the obvious sincerity behind his words held Landra's complete attention. Dr. Dyer cared, he really cared. His next words meant even more; she thought of Rose and Jimmy as he spoke.

"There are no families at Indian Camp, no natural, familial ties. Marriage between patients is absolutely prohibited, and if there are hapless couples who are confined there, they are forbidden to live with their spouses. Further, they are denied the right to vote in state and national elections, and our state law classes them among those afflicted with quarantinable, dangerously communicable diseases, such as Asiatic cholera, bubonic plague, and yellow fever!"

The dread words stirred up a buzz of excited conversation, and Dr. Dyer paused, then said, "The truth is, Hansen's disease is only mildly contagious, and only certain individuals contract it even if they're exposed, because it is highly probable that 90% of the whole human race is naturally immune to it! Only the simplest precautions are necessary—soap and water, and the normal rules of cleanliness."

At that, sudden shouts of disbelief arose, and he hastened to say, "It's true! Else why would there have been not a single person among the personnel or neighbors infected during the seven years the home in Indian Camp has been in existence? Think! Use your heads; stop this mindless, blind rush that is prompted by ignorance and superstition! It is absolutely essential that we move the facilities nearer; if it isn't done, if we don't have the assistance available at the University, we may never find a cure. Have you no compassion, no feeling for these poor, unfortunate individuals?"

He turned to Mr. Phelps. "Would it be possible for Dr. Jarrett to speak now, sir?"

"Of course. Dr. Jarrett, you have the floor."

Dyer sat down, a dejected slump in his shoulders that betrayed his fatigue.

Landra withdrew her hand as Adam stood. His tall, broad body towered beside her, and she wished desperately she could see his face more clearly. The outraged cries of the men seemed far away, as though she and Adam were in the smoke-hazed room alone. She barely heard the accusations some of them hurled. The only real thing was Adam's voice, starting slowly, then gathering in intensity as he spoke.

"In 1896, almost five years ago, my wife Bethany and I came to live at her family home, Greenlea. I had thought to teach, perhaps at Tulane University, and to carry on research begun in New York. We hadn't been in Jefferson Parish for long when my wife first began to suffer from . . . from certain symptoms which were beyond my knowledge as a physician. I consulted Dr. Dyer, whom I had good reason to trust and admire. We, my wife and I, hoped that the symptoms she was plagued with were the onset of a treatable, curable disease. There were many things it could have been. . . ."

Landra listened, her lips parted in shared misery as he named the diseases which doctors often mistakenly diagnose as leprosy:

"Dermal leishmaniasis, vitiligo, syringomyelia, Raynaud's Disease, Berhardt's Syndrome, facial paralysis, psoriasis, Lupus Vulgaris, sarcoid lupus, erythematosis, eczema, pellagra." The names rolled easily from his lips, like some kind of ritual incantation.

"But it was none of those. It was Hansen's disease—leprosy. We think it not only possible but probable that her body had harbored the bacillus for years before the symptoms manifested themselves. She was born and raised here in this part of the country, and Hansen's disease is endemic to the coastal south. We have no way of knowing where or how she contracted it." After a brief hesitation he continued, "Some time after Dr. Dyer's diagnosis, we found she was with child. It was during the months of her confinement that Dr. Dyer brought to my attention the pressing need of shelter for three of his patients, a young woman and two men. For reasons of their own, they were unwilling to go to the home at Indian Camp.

"By this time I was deeply committed to finding a more effective treatment for the disease, and thought perhaps to help them at the same time. My wife had need of another woman in the house, and since the two of them had their affliction in common, it seemed a good plan. I never meant to deceive the community; we were only trying to protect our patients. Some of you are aware that the Elkhorn property borders Greenlea, my home. I brought the Board of Control's attention to the fact that Elkhorn plantation house has stood empty for many years, and would serve admirably as a hospital."

He paused, his eyes sweeping the crowd. The angry muttering had not ceased during the time he was speaking, and the mood of those in the room was growing uglier by the minute.

"Don't you understand?" Adam began again. "If you deny the committee the right to proceed with the hospital at Elkhorn, if you continue to isolate these men and women from the skills and scientific knowledge at the School of Tropical Medicine at Tulane, you'll be responsible for setting back any progress toward the conquest of Hansen's bacillus for an incalculable amount of time! I beg you, don't do this!"

Dr. Stevens leaped to his feet, his voice raised in an agitated shout. "But you cannot expect us to stand idly by while you make it possible for those wretched creatures to walk among us . . . to be free to mix and mingle with those of us who are clean and untouched?"

Dr. Stevens turned to the crowd and said loudly, "Do you remember the story in the papers, before they were taken to Indian Camp, about the young man who served as cook for the others at the pesthouse on Hagan Avenue? He selected meat and vegetables from an open cart, handled them with his contaminated hands! Those very vegetables, those pieces of meat your unsuspecting wives may have bought, were fed to your children and you! Do we want to allow these people to roam unchecked on our streets?"

"No! No!" A chorus of angry voices shouted in answer. "Put them where they belong . . . keep them put away!"

Lucas had sat silent in his chair until now. He rose to speak, his voice cutting through the angry babble. "Wait, you're not being rational! I dare say there are those among you, perhaps the very man beside you, who are afflicted with syphillis, or tuberculosis. There's hardly a family in most of your acquaintances who has not been touched with the taint of one or both of these two diseases—yet the victims of both are allowed complete freedom. No one questions their right to complete, uninhibited social interaction with as many unsuspecting persons as they choose.

"We have told you, and rightly so, that Hansen's disease is feebly communicable, and then only in certain stages, and that most of you are probably naturally immune in any case. But syphillis and tuberculosis are both virulently contagious, and no one suggests those infected should be torn away from friends and family, to be made pariahs. It's wrong, surely you must see the error in such thinking—"

But his passionate argument was drowned out. One man, almost beside himself, shoved his way to within a few feet of the table where they sat. *"I say we finish the job—get rid of the whole lot!"*

His eyes were wide with a dazed frenzy, his face red. There was a small foam of spittle at the corner of his twisted mouth. To Landra's frightened eyes, he looked like a madman, as perhaps for the moment he was. She had no way of knowing he was a perfectly nice man who owned a delicatessen, who was much liked and revered by his customers and family.

At his inflammatory words, the crowd surged forward and Landra's stomach twisted in fear. Adam reached for her arm, and she barely heard him say to Lucas, "Get the carriage ready, quick! We'd better get her out of here, and in a hurry!"

She stumbled to her feet as he half pulled her from the chair. As they left, Adam caught Dr. Dyer's eye and he shook his head, his face creased in a worried frown. Lucas slipped out and she and Adam followed. The hallway was deserted, dim and shadowy, and just as they reached the back door she heard the crowd burst through in back of them; the stampede of many feet and many coarse, rage-filled voices filled the air.

"Adam!" she cried, "what are we going to do?"

"Get out of here as soon as possible. I said we were going to win, but we haven't! *We've lost . . .*"

Lucas had the carriage drawn as close to the side of the building as possible, and Adam leaped into it, pulling Landra with him. "Come on, Lucas, get going."

Even as he spoke the men who had been outside began to pour around the building, the word having spread quickly that the three of them had left the room. She saw, as the horses bounded forward at the slap of the whip in Lucas' hand, that they were at the door, the one who had shouted at Landra in the lead. He shook his fist at the now fast-moving carriage.

"You can't get away! We'll get you—we'll get you!"

Landra was grateful for the darkness of the carriage. She leaned against the seat, still trembling. When she had caught her breath she said softly, "Adam, you and Dr. Dyer were magnificent. I understand so much now that I didn't before."

He took a long time replying, and when he did his voice was tired, and held more than a hint of pain. "I should have taken the time to explain things more fully to you. I'm afraid you've been hurt badly by all this, and it's my fault. I do tend to be rather single-minded; and added to that I was thinking of you, ever since you came, as someone who would only hinder, not help."

"And now?"

"I've changed my mind." He sighed deeply, then said, "The other night, with Anson . . . I know you would have gone through with it if you'd had to. I never even thanked you. There's no excuse for the way I've been behaving. Can you forgive me?"

She stared at him in the darkness. "I—forgive *you*? It's you who'll have to forgive me, for not believing in you, for not standing by you!" She laid a hand on his arm.

"You did pretty well tonight, I'll have to say." He tried unsuccessfully to banish the pain in his tone. "I knew the odds were against us, but I never dreamed we'd be defeated so badly.

I shouldn't have brought you here tonight. It was a mistake."

"If you think you could have left me at home, you're sadly mistaken about that!" Suddenly she was aware that her hand, which she withdrew slowly, was wet. The warm stickiness was Adam's blood.

"Adam . . . your arm—"

"I must have started it bleeding when we got into the carriage a while ago. Lucas, where are we?"

"We're almost to the ferry. Can you hold out until we get across? I'm afraid if we don't, they might be right behind us."

"I can see to it," said Landra. "Do you have your bag in the carriage? I can shred my petticoat, but some sterile gauze would be better."

"You're right," Lucas agreed. "Yes, my bag is under the seat."

Quickly and with great tenderness Landra took the jacket from Adam's arm, only wincing for a second at the spreading redness that was making an ever-widening stain on his white sleeve. "Oh, Adam, why on earth didn't you wear the sling?"

"I didn't want them to think . . . to think I was badly hurt. I thought—"

She shook her head. "Sometimes you don't think very well at all." She packed and bound the wound once more, improvising a makeshift sling to help support the injured arm.

"Thank you," Adam murmured. He didn't speak again. In the silence Landra was able to marshal her scattered thoughts, to whip them into some semblance of order. It was no small task; for being present tonight at the council meeting, however much a failure it had been for Dyer and Adam and Lucas, had made her aware of a great many things which had puzzled her in the weeks since she'd come to Louisiana.

There was no difficulty in choosing which of the two opposing sides held the lion's share of truth. Being her father's daughter made her extremely wary of men who cannot present their case without rabid emotionalism. The opposition had failed to impress her in any way. On the other hand, Dr. Dyer had calmly and convincingly presented a case that would have made sense to every man in the room had they not been under the influence of the mob. What a curious, frightening thing was a mob! Separately they were sane, reasonable men; together, they were a raging, ugly thing. She shivered involuntarily and drew closer to Adam.

CHAPTER 19

As Landra had fully expected, the house was dark. She thought with a sudden pang that the three within were the most concerned, yet they were the ones forced to wait endlessly while others decided their fate. Lucas had returned to New Orleans to see if Dyer was all right, and Landra followed as Adam went quickly to the lab. Jimmy and Rose sat close together on the cot, her hand held tightly in his. Hollis, quiet except for a murmured greeting to Landra, watched as Adam went to Anson.

There seemed to be no difficulty in his breathing this evening, but the tape encircling his neck and the shining silver tube protruding from the incision only added to the horror of his appearance. Was it imagination and hope, or were the ugly red welts on his forehead a little lighter in color—could it be that the recession of symptoms was, even now, coming about?

Rose tried to smile, but failed. "Dr. Adam, is it . . . was—"

The hard line of Adam's mouth was worse than ever. "Rose, I don't know how to tell you this."

"You don't have to," she said, her tone flat and expressionless now. "They won't allow us to go to Elkhorn, will they?"

"I can't even tell you that for certain. All I can say is that public opposition is even worse than we suspected. The council wasn't able to reach a decision. Lucas, Landra and I left before it was over. Most of those present were totally irrational."

"I understand," Rose said softly.

"Well," said Jimmy, "I don't! They say we're dangerous—it's them that are the animals! They're the ones that ought to be driven out, not us."

"Jimmy, don't. It won't do any good." Rose tried to calm him

184

but he wrenched away and stood, swaying uncertainly.

"Let me alone! There's nothing else left to me, at least let me get mad!" He had a black band wrapped around his eyes, and as he took a step forward he bumped into a chair and fell heavily to his knees. A sob was torn from his throat and Anson came over to him, offering his arm which Jimmy took hold of and straightened up with effort. "What are we going to do, Anson? What are we going to do?" Though he could not speak, Anson's empathy was obvious.

Landra was awed at the depth of feeling between the two men, men who were bound together by a bond she had never before seen. Hollis, finally fully aware of the extent of their plight, had gone to Landra. He said nothing as he stood close, but both drew strength from the other's nearness. And they all looked to Adam for direction. She said softly to him, "I'll go and make some tea, Adam—"

"No, you'd better pack, just in case," he replied in a whisper. "I've no idea how far that mob will go, but it won't hurt to be prepared."

Shaken, she nodded and left the room, after Hollis kissed her cheek quickly and murmured in her ear, "I'm here, we're all together . . . don't be afraid."

Just as she was about to go upstairs, she heard a knock at the front door, a light tap at first, then louder and louder. She hesitated. Was it safe to answer the door, or should she get Adam? Chiding herself for being afraid, she opened it and found Sam'l there, his hands twisting his hat nervously.

"Why, Sam'l, what are you doing here?"

"Dr. Adam done tole me to cum and tell him if anything or anybody cum to Elkhorn. Well, they's there, all right, and they done burn the whole thing—it's burnin' right now! And that ain't all. I heard 'em say they're comin' here!"

Not wanting to believe him, Landra stepped out onto the veranda and looked toward the river. There it was, the faint, rosy glow of a fire, a big one. "Oh, Sam'l," she breathed. "You weren't hurt . . . they didn't hurt you, did they?"

"Oh no, ma'am, I din't let 'em see me."

Frightened, Landra said, "I'd better tell Adam. We may not have much time!"

"Yes'm, I'm afeared all you folks better git out of here, and mighty quick. You 'member I tole you that was a awful strong gris gris. I done my best to git rid of it, but hit shore looks like I din't make it!"

Landra squeezed the old man's thin arm for an instant. "I know you tried, Sam'l, and we're grateful. Come with me to find Dr. Jarrett."

He rolled his eyes and shook his head. "If hit's all the same to you, ma'am, I'll jest wait out chere. I got to be gittin' on down the road. Think I'll go on to my sister's, if Dr. Adam don't need me no more."

"You wait right here, and I'll get him." Landra hurried back to the lab, and as Adam followed her to where Sam'l waited, she told him the news he had brought.

"I was afraid of something like this. I'll give Sam'l the grey and the small carriage. He'll be better off the farther away he gets from Greenlea. I shouldn't have let Lucas leave. Well, at least your young doctor is with us."

The old man protested, but finally allowed Adam to persuade him to take the small rig. When he climbed in he said, "I'll send it back directly, Dr. Adam, don't you worry none 'bout this rig. Soon's I git to my sister's over in Bogalusa I'll have her boy bring it back. I surely do thank you."

"No, Sam'l, it's you we ought to thank. You'd better be on your way before they get here." There was a note of urgency in his tone as he glanced down the drive.

"I'm mighty sorry, Dr. Adam. If they's something I could do—"

"No, there's nothing, except to leave now; we'll have to do the same. Good-bye, Samuel Burton, my friend. I hope I see you again. Thank you for helping us."

Sam'l nodded his head, and Landra reached out and grasped his hand in hers for a second. "Good-bye, Sam'l, and Godspeed. Be careful, won't you?"

"Yes'm, I will."

He clucked to the horse and they set off at a brisk pace down the drive. Landra watched for a couple of seconds, then turned to Adam. "What do you want me to do?"

"Get Rose and Jimmy ready, and I'll see to Anson. I have to get my notes, and enough medicine to last until we can get them to Indian Camp."

"It's come to that, then?"

"There's nothing else we can do. If they—" He stopped as he

saw a figure approaching the house. "Get inside, quick!" he said, his voice low in warning.

"It's me, Dr. Jarrett, it's Denis!"

"Denis!" called Landra. "What are you doing here?"

He came up, a little breathless, as he said, "I brought Carrie and the baby, because she was awful worried after we heard the news about what happened at the council meeting. They're over by the road."

"Good lord, man, they're burning Elkhorn now! We can't have them here when that mob gets here. I'll go talk to her."

Without asking, Landra followed Adam as he strode toward the buggy. Carrie leaned out. She held the baby, his eyes bright with excitement, his little body wrapped snugly in a blanket. He gurgled happily as he saw Adam, who took him from her and held him close.

"Whatever possessed you to come here? There's a mob at Elkhorn, and they may be already headed this way. They might not stop even at harming a child. Didn't I tell you to put him first?"

"I had to see you. I was afraid you would leave without coming—" She faltered, and saw that Landra was standing quietly beside Adam. "I didn't mean to make more trouble for you, Adam."

"You must take Rob back to your house immediately and look after him until we can send for him. Can you . . . will you do that for me?" His voice was anxious, and he kept looking down the river road for some sign of trouble.

"I'd keep him forever, you know that. Adam, let me go with you! Don't leave me behind; take Rob and me with you, please!" She looked at Landra and Denis, as if ashamed of pleading, then grasped Adam's arm, not caring whether they saw or not. "I don't want to stay if you aren't here."

Knowing full well that an angry mob of men might momentarily appear in the bend of the road, Adam caught Rob to him closely for one long minute, then handed him back to Carrie. Still he did not speak.

Landra felt the woman's pain; how could she bear it if she were Carrie? She stepped close to the carriage and kissed the baby on his soft cheek. "I'll go and make sure the others are ready to leave, Adam. Good-bye, Carrie; I can never thank you enough for what you've done for Rob." She found the words easy to say, for they were true.

She had not gone many steps when Denis caught up with her. "Miss Cole, Landra . . . I may not see you again, and I wanted to tell you—" He stopped, then burst out, "I'm awfully sorry for the way Katy acted! You mustn't think there isn't anything, anything at all we wouldn't do to help you. Mama said for me to tell you if there was anything she could ever do, for you to come to her straight off. You will, won't you?"

"Of course, Denis. Tell Rene I appreciate her kindness, and I'll never forget any of you." She thought for a second, then reached up and unclasped a small locket that hung around her neck. "Give this to Jeannette, will you? And tell her thank you for sharing her room with me."

"I sure will," Denis said earnestly. "Take care, Landra."

"Don't worry about me, Denis. Good-bye," she said as he turned and went back to the carriage where Adam was talking to Carrie. The waning moonlight was kind to the sad, peeling exterior of Greenlea. How her mother would have been hurt at the sight of it. Landra was glad she had never seen it like this, never known about Bethany. It had been her sister's wish, and she now understood Bethany's deception with the letters.

Rose was waiting anxiously just inside the door. "I heard what Sam'l said; are they coming? What are we going to do?"

As confidently as possible, Landra said, "Get your things together, Rose. We have to leave."

"Where are we going?"

It was very hard to meet the girl's eyes. "To Indian Camp."

"No! I won't go there! Jimmy and I will run away . . ."

"Jimmy needs medical treatment, and you know it. It would be a miracle if you found another doctor who would be as sympathetic as Adam. You have to face the facts, Rose." Landra did not want to be so blunt, but she felt the urgency of time. "Where are Anson and Jimmy?"

"They're waiting in the back with Dr. Freman," said Rose dully.

"Are they ready to leave?"

"Yes. What have we got to get ready? All Anson is taking, except what's on his back, is his book. And Jimmy has barely spoken since you came. It's as though he's given up, like—"

"My sister? Well, we aren't going to give up, at least I'm not. How about you?"

Rose pulled her pink shawl closer about her shoulders. "If we have to go, we have to go. You're right about Jimmy needing

Dr. Jarrett; I'd forgotten for a minute. Whatever happens, I guess I can stand it."

"Of course you can, Rose. Both of us have to be strong, whether we think we can or not. God will give us the strength we need." She knew there would be a time when Rose would be able to accept the truth that Landra was finding more and more comforting with each passing moment. There would be a time she could share it with Rose, and, God willing, Jimmy. She said softly, "If . . . if it helps, Rose, I'll be with you."

The girl's eyes grew wide. "You mean at Indian Camp? You'd go there when you don't have to? Why?"

"Because I believe I have something to offer, as a nurse. I've decided it's what I want to do with my life." At Rose's reaction, one of amazed disbelief, she added honestly and humbly, "Hollis . . . Dr. Freman, is convinced we can both help. He and I love each other, Rose."

She looked at Landra for a long moment, then a small, tremulous smile lightened her face. "I see. Thank you for telling me. It . . . it does help."

"Good. Now, let's make sure Jimmy and Anson are ready. Adam will be here any minute with the carriage. I left him with Denis Chaumont and Carrie."

They found Jimmy and Anson huddled close to the side of the stable. Anson's eyes were watching the glow in the sky, the sad signal of the death of a dream. Iberville Parish was a long, long way from New Orleans. Anson dePaul knew full well he would never see his family again, not even from the painful distance that had separated them in the past six years. Never again would he see his beloved Marie; the thought that she had lain in the arms of another man, had borne him a son, hit him afresh, and he barely suppressed a low groan. The book. There was always the book. He held it tightly to his chest. If it were published, it might give the world a glimpse of what it meant to be a leper—the anguish, the absolute separation from the world that no man should impose upon another—and perhaps his life would have meaning, after all. His mind stumblingly phrased a prayer . . . a prayer that somehow God would allow this to happen, and he clung to the belief that it would be so.

Adam came running toward them then and said, "The carriage is around front. I'm afraid we've about run out of time. Come on, hurry!" There was a note of extreme urgency, of fear, even, in his voice. But Landra knew it was fear for them, not himself. He was responsible for the four of them, and that responsibility weighed heavily on him.

"Hollis! Adam, where is Hollis?"

"He's still inside, Landra, packing some things for me. He's not going to be in the carriage; we felt it was best if he rides separately on horseback."

"But why?"

"Let's just say it's best that way, safer. He'll not be far behind, I assure you. Please, let's get them together."

Though her anxiety deepened, she did as she was told, knowing Adam did not really mean to shut her out, that he was simply unaccustomed to sharing information with her; she was a woman, therefore, she should be protected instead of burdened. The same as before the council meeting . . . and just as hard to bear. She helped the others into the carriage; Rose and Jimmy huddled together in the backseat, Anson in the far corner, his precious book clutched tightly against his chest. Worriedly, Landra listened to the sound of his breathing. Was it her imagination, or was it more labored?

When she whispered the question to Adam he said, "It's the pressure, the excitement. When we get him to Indian Camp, there'll be time for him to heal. He has a lot of resistance, or he wouldn't be alive now." He turned to Anson. "I think you'd better stay completely out of sight, Anson, in the event that we do meet any of them. If they were to see you, they might be frightened by the tube. Fear begets rage, and we can't afford to take chances. All right?" Anson nodded at Adam's suggestion.

As they reached the end of the oyster-shell drive, Landra peered down the dark road. There was no one in sight. However, she had barely let out a small sigh of relief when a harsh voice called out. "Stop! Don't go any farther!" To back up his order, a man sprang from behind the tree at the left of the carriage. He grabbed the reins, jerking them and causing the horses to shy wildly. The man was almost lifted from his feet, but he hung on. "Tom!" he shouted. "Get over here—they're trying to leave!"

As if from nowhere three men appeared, and as Landra watched in terror, they lit torches and stood in a solid line across the entrance to the road that led to town. The wildly dancing firelight made the faces of the men appear distorted and unreal.

"Let us pass!" called Adam, but he was answered by loud shouts of denial and derision.

"Not on your life! The others will be here soon. We'd do the job now, but we promised we'd wait and let everybody in on the finish!" It was the man who'd grabbed the horses who spoke. He still held the reins firmly in his hand.

A sound of horses reached their ears, and one of the men shouted, "There they come!"

Realizing it might be the only chance they would have, Adam took the seldom-used whip from its niche at the side of the carriage and struck at the man holding the horses. Grimly he lashed out repeatedly, hoping to startle the man into letting go. Landra pressed her hands over her mouth, suppressing the scream that rose in her throat.

With an oath the man dropped the reins and snatched the whip. "Grab on, Tom, let's pull this leper-lover out and do him in once and for all!"

The man called Tom handed his torch to one of the other men, and the two of them yanked Adam from the carriage.

"Adam!" cried Landra.

But Adam couldn't answer, could not even hear. He hit his head on the edge of the wheel as he fell and lay limp on the ground. Landra stared in horror for an endless moment, then climbed over the seat and dropped to the ground beside him.

His face was pale in the flickering firelight, but she could see a tiny pulse beating in his temple. There was no blood. *Hollis, where was Hollis? Surely he would come in a moment!* "Adam, *Adam*! Please, wake up—"

"Oh, Adam, please wake up!" mimicked one of the men. "Take my word for it, sis, it'd be better for him if he don't!"

As the riders, most of whom were carrying torches, drew near, he called out to them. "We already got one of 'em, the doctor."

"Hey, Tom, you told us you'd wait! That ain't fair."

"There's still a whole buggy full of 'em. Look there!" He came close and shoved the torch into the interior of the carriage. Rose and Jimmy shrank back, and Anson quietly slid to the floor, trying desperately to keep out of sight as Adam had instructed him.

"What are we going to do?" shouted one of the men.

It was a question that made Landra hold her breath. What, indeed, were they going to do? With as much courage as she could muster she said, "Let us go, we mean you no harm—"

But they would not allow her to finish. "You aren't going

anywhere! Once and for all, we're going to rid this parish of all of you!" The man they called Tom came close enough for her to smell the whiskey on his breath. She pulled Adam's dark, unconscious head closer, but stood her ground as he said loudly, "Hey, I'll take care of this little gal here; you fellas can handle the rest!"

"We've had enough talk. Let's get on with it, here and now!" There was a murmur of assent, and they all surged forward.

"No, leave us alone!" Landra cried. "The law, the police—someone will know you . . . you murdered us. You can't get away with it!"

Tom said, "She's right, boys. We'd better be a little smarter. There wasn't anybody in the house over at Elkhorn. How's anybody to know if there was anybody here at Greenlea? All we have to do is put them in the house and do a repeat. Right?"

"Right! If it burns, how'll they prove there was anybody in it? We've got plenty of kerosene, plenty of fire!" The man who spoke brandished his torch, and all the others shouted and waved theirs as well.

Landra looked at the fire-lit faces, searching for a sane, reasonable expression, but there was none. To a man every one was afflicted with a disease almost equal in its devastating powers to that within the carriage—the disease of blind, totally unreasonable, prejudiced fear.

Hopelessly she clutched Adam to her, her eyes shut tight against what was surely coming, and she missed seeing what caused the men to draw back suddenly, a spate of frightened oaths spilling from their mouths.

"Holy Mother of God . . . look at him!"

"His face, look at his face!"

"He's one of them!"

Holding her breath, Landra looked up. There, in the front of the carriage, standing as straight and tall as he was physically able, was Anson dePaul. The firelight shone on the hideous welts that covered his forehead and nose; his eyes were black gaping holes that shone darkly with fever—and something else. Clutched in his claw-like hands was the precious manuscript, which he slowly lifted up and toward the crowd.

"Look! What's he got? What is it?"

A harsh, croaking sound came from Anson's throat as he strained to speak. His breathing was quite rapid now, and one of the men caught sight of the shining silver tube which protruded from his neck.

"What's that thing in his neck? He's got a thing in his neck! Look at him! He's not like a real man; he's a monster . . . a monster!" Fear stuck the words in the man's throat, but they were still recognizable. The others took up the cry.

"A monster! He's a monster, kill him, kill him!" They chanted it over and over until one of them threw the torch he held and struck Anson full in the chest. He staggered, then fell to the ground. With an animal-like snarl, one of the men hit the fallen man again and again.

The fear suddenly, miraculously left Landra. She released Adam, who sat dazedly, still on the edge of consciousness, and ran over to where Anson lay. The crazed man stopped in the very act of raising his torch once more to strike Anson. She stood defiantly in his way.

"If you intend to hit him again, you'll have to kill me first," she said. "Do you want to kill a woman face to face as well as a fine man like Anson? He's a man, not a monster—don't you see, he's a man!"

With a calmness that seemed impossible she knelt beside Anson. From the silver tube came a faint rustle of sound, the faint hope of life. It was possible only for her to hear it because quite suddenly, there was absolute quiet. The men watched as she bent her head close to his and begged, "Anson, don't die, please don't die!" He was trying to speak, and Landra was all the more distressed, for she knew he could not. "What? Oh, Anson, I can't understand!" Then, one of the ugly clawed hands scrabbled in the shell of the drive, reaching for the scattered pages. She understood finally, and began to gather them up. "I'll see to it for you, Anson, I promise. Don't worry."

He nodded once, and she sat in the powder dust, his ruined head cradled in her lap. It was not many seconds before there was no sound whatever from the silver tube, no movement from the body which had been wracked with such misery.

Landra looked up at the circle of faces. "Are you satisfied? He's dead . . . oh, he's dead!" The tears rolled down her face, and no matter how much she told herself Anson was better off, that he was with God, there was no helping the utter sadness that filled her.

Slowly she lowered his head to the ground and gathered the remainder of the carefully written pages, all that was left in the world of Anson dePaul. She knew full well that he had disobeyed Adam's orders in order to give the rest of them a chance. He had wanted his life to count, to mean something.

Oh, Anson, she mourned; *it did mean something, it did.*

CHAPTER 20

There was little time for mourning. As Landra gathered up the last of the papers, she jerked her head up at the sound of a horse, from the direction of the house.

"Not more of them, Lord," she prayed; "not more." With a glad rush of relief she saw Hollis swing down and come running over to her.

"What's going on?" he cried, as he took in the scene. "Oh, Landra, I'm sorry I wasn't here . . . Adam asked me to—" He broke off, his fierce gaze on the men who hung sullenly back, scowls replacing the madness of a moment before. "Have they hurt you?" Hollis placed an arm around her shoulders and she sagged against him gratefully.

"No, but . . . Anson, he's dead, and Adam—" She started to rise and go to him.

"Wait just a moment. Get in the carriage; I'll see to Adam. What happened?"

"Two of the men pulled him down, and he hit his head."

Hollis quickly helped her up into the carriage and went around to check on Adam, ignoring the angry buzz of voices from the men. Adam was conscious now, and just able to step up and take his place beside Landra. She noticed he was still alarmingly pale. "Will he be all right?" she asked Hollis anxiously.

"I think so, if there's no concussion. You'd better get out of here, because we've no guarantee that bunch won't decide to finish what they started. Do you think you can manage the horses?" His hand clasped hers tightly.

"Yes, but what about Anson?"

"I'll see to him, then catch up with you." For a moment he

was silent; then he said softly, "I love you. Be careful."

"I don't want to leave you!" For answer he slapped the horse nearest him and started them moving. For a long, agonizing moment it looked as though the milling, murmuring crowd of men would stop her, and her heart thumped almost audibly in her breast.

Hollis mounted his horse. "Let her through; you've done enough! *Let them through!*"

They fell back, momentarily startled by his authoritative shout. It was enough to allow the horses to pass through and beyond to the road. Once there, she clumsily, inexpertly urged on the team of horses. Still frightened from the torches, they were quite skittish, and she was having a great deal of trouble keeping them on the road. Adam reached over and took the reins from her.

Although she was grateful, she glanced at him sharply. "Are you all right?"

"I will be after we put some miles between us and them." His voice was stronger, and she relaxed a little, though not much. She kept looking back, expecting them to follow. Rose and Jimmy were absolutely silent, Rose's great sad eyes staring, almost as unseeing as Jimmy's.

It was not until they had passed through Noirville and come to the ferry dock that Adam spoke again. "Landra, we'll have to work something out. I can't take Rose and Jimmy into the city. Someone might see them, and after what's happened, we can't take any more chances. Somehow we have to get you to a safe place to wait until you can book passage to New York." Evidently the night air had cleared away what remained of his dizziness, for he sounded almost normal.

"I'm not going back to New York," she said steadily.

"But—"

He was interrupted by a shout from a horseman who was waiting by the small ferry. "Dr. Jarrett!"

Adam drew the horses to a halt and peered cautiously into the darkness. "Yes, who is it?"

"It's me, Lucas." He came alongside the carriage and looked back at Rose and Jimmy. "Where is Anson?"

"He's dead," said Rose, her voice catching on the words. "They killed him, and they would have killed us, too . . ."

"I . . . I'm sorry," said Lucas helplessly. "I should never have left. Dyer got out of the building soon after we did, and he's all right. I heard about the plans for burning Elkhorn, and decided to wait for you here. I had no idea they would include Greenlea, too. I just thought you'd probably leave right away, and . . . oh, I'm really sorry about Anson."

Adam, his mouth drawn in the old, familiar hard line, said, "I want to ask a favor of you, Lucas. Before you leave for Indian Camp, I wonder if you would be responsible for seeing that Landra gets out of the city safely, that she gets on the train or steamship to New York?"

"Yes, of course I will," he answered quickly. "Only . . . only I won't be going to Indian Camp, Dr. Jarrett."

The two men looked at each other for a moment; then Adam asked, "Why not, if I may ask?"

"It's not a hasty decision; for months now, ever since her death, I've been thinking about it."

"You mean my wife."

Lucas nodded. "I just don't feel I can comfortably work with you any longer. It's not all your fault, I realize that. But it's no less a fact. I find myself blaming you for—" He cleared his throat, a painful sound. "Anyway, it's no good anymore. I can't do my job, can't keep my mind on my work. And now, with Elkhorn gone, all our work ruined, don't you see, I have to find a place for myself, free from the past!"

Adam nodded slowly. "I accept your decision, even understand it. Good luck." He looked at the other man steadily, then said, "Now, will you take care of Landra for me? Somehow I have to get Jimmy and Rose to a safe place."

"I'm going with you, Adam; Hollis and I both are," said Landra. "Lucas, thank you just the same, but I won't be going back to New York. I hope you find what you're looking for."

"Landra, please!" said Adam. "You can't go with me. I don't even know for sure where I'm going!"

"Nevertheless, wherever it is, I'm going, too. Lucas, I know it's asking a lot, but will you go back to Greenlea and make sure Hollis is all right, and tell him we're waiting for him here? He has to . . . he'll need help with Anson's body. And I'm not even sure he's all right—" She'd started bravely; at the thought of the mob and Hollis alone she couldn't go on.

"Of course I will." Lucas hesitated for an instant, then wheeled his horse and was gone.

Adam rubbed his aching head. "Landra, Dr. Freman is young and inexperienced, and you're headstrong and inexperienced.

Neither of you has the least idea of what lies ahead. You aren't thinking logically. Have you forgotten if you go to Indian Camp, you'll be constantly exposed to the same thing that killed Bethany?"

Quietly she answered. "Have *you* forgotten Dr. Dyer's speech tonight? He said it's only mildly contagious, and simple precautions such as washing with soap and water are all that's necessary." She glanced back into the dark interior of the carriage. "Oh, I do hope Hollis won't be too long coming. I'm afraid the night dampness will be bad for Jimmy."

"Your concern for Jimmy is touching, but you don't seem to realize—"

"And you don't seem to realize that someone besides you can be concerned! I care about Jimmy, and Rose, and I cared about Anson . . ." She faltered, then lifted her chin. "Dr. Atwood always said I was a natural nurse. With a little training, I can be a good one. I know it. Surely the sisters at Indian Camp would welcome my help. I should think an offer of help from any quarter would be welcome. Adam, you're the one who isn't thinking logically. You've been shot, attacked by a mob, possibly have a concussion, and you're going to need help making sure Rose and Jimmy reach Indian Camp. Whether you can admit it or not, you need us."

Stubbornly he countered, "You don't know what you're saying. It's dirty, back-breaking work, and only the fanatically dedicated can even survive, much less live decently. There is certainly no place for false pity in those who work with these people."

"Is that what you think I'm feeling, false pity?"

"Well, true pity is one of the rarest, most tender and precious of emotions. However, human nature being what it is, pity is often corrupted into something which comes from a desire for self-satisfaction instead of real compassion."

"Oh, Adam, Hollis can't hold a candle to you when it comes to being pompous! Are you questioning my motives?"

"No, it's just that I've seen people who do things for the 'poor lepers' in order to get some kind of special reward, from God as well as their fellowmen. Do you know there's even a special mission to the lepers? Not to the tubercular, or the diabetics, or the syphilitic, however. It seems there's a feeling that a person who devotes his life to lepers gets special blessings or something."

"I don't know about all that. All I know is, that for the first time in my life, I feel so deeply about something, I want to give whatever I am as a person to it; or in this case, to fighting it." She paused, then said slowly, "Why are *you* doing it, Adam? Is guilt any more acceptable a motive?"

She was immediately sorry for her question when she heard the deep weariness in his voice as he answered. "Let's stop sniping at each other's motives. I . . . I'm willing to accept your help, for whatever reason you offer it. It's going to be a long, hard pull. After tonight there seems to be no alternative other than Indian Camp, with all its problems."

"But with all the problems, Adam, there is a glimmer of hope down the way. Our heavenly Father is with us and He will show us how to help these people—even in Indian Camp!"

Adam smiled in spite of himself. "Yes, and someday there may be even a cure . . ." His voice trailed off and a shadow darkened his eyes as he stared down at the reins still clutched in his hands.

"What about Rob, Adam? and Carrie?" Landra's voice brought him back to the present.

He waited a long while before he said, "No one is aware Rob is my son except Denis Chaumont. I'm not sure if his family knows, though," he added uncertainly.

"Denis would not have told anyone, not even his mother," said Landra, remembering that young man's aversion to gossip. "The secret is safe with him, I'm sure."

"And I have to believe Rob is safe with Carrie. We don't know what we'll find at Indian Camp, or how long it will be before I can send for them."

"You intend to have Carrie come, too, then? I could take care of Rob, Adam."

"I'm certainly not doubting your ability to take care of him. It's just that, well, I simply cannot take him away from her. She loves him so."

His face was shadowed and Landra could not read the expression there. "And what about you, Adam; you know she loves you desperately. Do you think you can ever return that love?"

Adam stared into the darkness. "I don't know, Landra, I just don't know. All I feel now is emptiness. Emptiness when I think of Bethany, when I think of how everything we've worked for is done, finished, literally up in smoke. It may be a long time, if ever, before I feel anything again."

Softly Landra said, "I have an idea Carrie will wait, Adam. And . . ." She swallowed, and the next words came hard. "Between the two of us, Carrie and I will see that Rob is well cared for."

"Yes," he said, "we'll send for them as soon as we're settled and have a safe place for them." He still sounded just a bit shaky as he put a hand to his head. "It's getting cool. Would you see if those two are cold? There are some blankets under the seat."

"Of course, Adam," she said, glad for something to do. Rose and Jimmy were almost asleep, held tightly in each other's arms. She felt a stab of fear for them; what lay ahead? Was there any hope of some kind of normal life for them, some happiness? Landra decided right then that there would be. Someday Rose and Jimmy would know her God; someday they would be married and have a home together. Tenderly she tucked the carriage robe around them.

She did not voice her growing concern for Hollis; Adam had enough on his mind. But it weighed heavily on hers, and with a little rush of gladness she heard the sound of hoofbeats, coming fast. "It's Hollis!"

She was halfway out of the carriage when Adam said, "Wait, it might not be him—"

But she *knew* it was! He swung down from the horse almost before the animal had fully halted, and Landra flung herself joyfully into his waiting arms. "Are you all right? I was worried; I tried not to think of what they might do to you—" He stopped her words with his lips on hers; she clung to him, secure in his strength.

When he finally drew away he said, his breath soft against her cheek, "It seems like forever since I saw you drive away."

"That's because it has been!" Landra laughed shakily. "I hope I never, never have to leave you like that again."

"Then don't." He kissed her again. "You will marry me, won't you, when we get to wherever it is we're going? On the way here, I realized I hadn't even asked."

"Yes, yes!" It was Landra this time who tightened her arms around his neck and drew his head to meet hers. "You're going to think I'm not a lady if I keep being so . . . so abandoned."

He sighed, his cheek on her hair. "Whatever you call it, don't stop. I like you . . . no, I love you, just the way you are."

"Adam used to say I was as transparent as a clean windowpane. I never could hide my feelings, even when I was a girl."

"I love it! You're wonderful, like a breath of fresh air . . ." He would have kissed her again but Adam's voice, quiet and low with strain, came from the carriage.

"I hate to interrupt, but it's a very long way to Indian Camp. We'd best be going."

One quick, last kiss, and Hollis whispered in her ear, "Remember, love, no matter what's ahead, what we have to face, if we're together, we can make it."

Landra nodded wordlessly as he lifted her into the carriage beside Adam, then went to tie his horse behind.

When he returned and came to sit on the other side of her, Adam gave over the reins to him without a word. As the carriage moved into the darkness, Landra felt the most extraordinary mixture of feelings. Grief, when she thought of Anson and the two behind them; apprehension at the unknown future; boundless love for the man beside her—and absolute assurance that God traveled with them.

A sequel to this story is available
at your local Christian bookstore,
To Make the Bitter Sweet.

Epilogue

The hospital whose troubled origins I recounted in the preceding story is now housed in 100 buildings located on 325 acres at Carville, Louisiana, upriver from New Orleans. Although this is the only U.S. Public Health Service Hospital for the treatment of Hansen's disease in this country, besides the one in Hawaii, the number of cases is not getting smaller, but larger. Immigrants already suffering with leprosy have increased the cases reported (as of January 1983) to more than 4,000. This represents a rise of almost 500% since 1960, and the social stigma is far from gone. Some doctors still caution their newly diagnosed patients not to tell anyone what they have, lest they become social outcasts, lose their jobs, or even worse, are shunned by their own families.

Since the 1940s leprosy has been treated with dapsone, a safe, inexpensive sulfone drug which arrests the disease and prevents contagion. There are other helpful drugs, but they have undesirable side effects and are expensive. Doctors are concerned because many patients seem to be developing a resistance to dapsone; the ultimate answer, of course, lies in a vaccine. Currently, armadilloes, which are among the few animals susceptible to leprosy, are being used in the research to develop such a vaccine. Early results are encouraging, but because of the slow incubation of the disease, no real solutions can be expected for a decade or more.

So there is still no cure, although many of the deformities, such as "claw hands," can now be corrected by surgery. Probably the most realistic answer lies in the philosophy of the doctors at Carville, who believe treated patients can and should be returned to society as independent, wage-earning, tax-paying citizens. Those doctors are diligently working toward that end.